My Mom the Miracle

1 Woman, 2 Cancers, 3 Years, 4-Ever Grateful

Ashley Hahn Calvery

DEDICATION

First and foremost, this book is dedicated to my family. Mom and Dad, I will never forget our theme song, "Just the three of us, we can make it if we try!" We sure made it! We've been through a lot! I love you guys :).

Also, this is for all of the people battling cancer and their loved ones; you too can beat this! Remember to stay positive, set goals (both short and long term), pray, and surround yourself with encouraging, supportive and upbeat people.

To all of the doctors, nurses and caregivers, you all are underappreciated. A special shout out to Ruby Memorial Hospital, Dr. Craig, Dr. Abraham, the whole Bone Marrow Unit "crew," Dr. Capelle, Dr. Ashraf and the Mary Babb Cancer Center. We love you guys. Thanks for joining "Team Hahn" and saving my mom's life!

Thank you to all of those who prayed. The prayers got us to where we are today. Our family and friends, their family and friends, as well as complete strangers known as our "prayer warriors," all prayed for my mom.

This is also dedicated to all of those who came to help care for Mom during our time of need. Although my father and I were the primary caregivers when my mother was sick, we had several family members and friends reach out to support us. They came to stay with Mom when my dad was traveling and the few times I had to get back home to Maryland throughout the battle. My brother Matt, my husband Brian, my mom's brother Tim, my dad's sister Cathy, my dad's brother Jim, my cousin Julie, my mom's good friends Cher and Joni, all of our neighbors on our street, and even my friends Heather, Lisa and Laurie all took time out of their busy schedules to come and be with us. Thank you. We couldn't have gotten through all of this without you guys.

ABOUT THE AUTHOR

When you pick up this book to read it, please know that I am not someone who ever planned to write a book. It just happened. It is apparent in some of the language that I have used that I simply decided to start typing one day, and over several months a story had unfolded. A story about an amazing woman who happens to be my mother.

I graduated from the University of Maryland with a bachelor's degree in Early Childhood Education. Go Terps! Since graduating, I have taught kindergarten in Maryland and Florida. I took a year off of work to care for my mom, who is not only my mother, but also a best friend! Since then, I earned my masters degree as a Reading Teacher from the University of Loyola in Maryland. Go Greyhounds!

I am very close with my family and have recently gotten married to the man of my dreams. I do not mention him nearly enough in this book, but every other weekend, he drove three hours each way to come visit me, and every single day, probably ten times a day, we talked on the phone. Some of the weekends he visited, we spent our time simply staring at each other in a hospital room; while others he helped with Mom around the house. He was amazing during this whole process. Anyone could have left someone to go through this alone, but he was right by my side, every step of the way. My hubby and I reside in Florida (recent move) and hope within the next few years to start a family of our own.

Please note that embedded throughout this book are all of the emails that were sent as progress reports to our family and friends. They have not been changed or edited. I felt as though if I corrected them, then it would take away from the emotions I felt as I passionately typed each of them out to update everyone on Mom's battle.

CONTENTS

Acknowledgments

1   Cancer #1   Pg 1

2   Our Celebration Comes to a Halt   Pg 3

3   Prepared; But for What?   Pg 7

4   Communication   Pg 9

5   August 2008- Are You Kidding Me?   Pg 13

6   September 2008- Cancer #2 Battle Continues   Pg 20

7   October 2008- Mom Hates October   Pg 30

8   November 2008- Thanksgiving in Vegas   Pg 37

9   December 2008- The Holidays   Pg 40

10   January 2009- Preparing For Our Big Day   Pg 45

11   February 2009- Transplant Month   Pg 48

12   March 2009- March Madness?   Pg 56

13   April 2009- Amazing Friends and Family   Pg 66

14   May 2009- We Reach the 100th Day   Pg 72

15   June 2009- Summertime   Pg 76

16   July 2009- Mom's 42nd Birthday (Wink, Wink)   Pg 80

17   August 2009- Ash Says Goodbye   Pg 85

18   September 2009- A Visit to WV   Pg 94

19   October 2009- Eye Trouble   Pg 98

20   November 2009- Back In the Stands   Pg 103

21   December 2009- Holidays to Celebrate   Pg 105

22   January 2010- A New Year   Pg 108

23   February 2010- Happy 1st Birthday Mom   Pg 111

24   March 2010- NCAA Tourney Watch Out   Pg 114

25   May 2010- My Big Day   Pg 117

26   June 2010- Road to a Normal Life Again   Pg 123

27   July and August 2010- First Summer Post-Transplant   Pg 125

28   Fall After Transplant   Pg 128

29   Winter   Pg 130

30   A New Beginning   Pg 134

ACKNOWLEDGMENTS

Aunt Linda, Aunt Ann and Brian, thank you for reading this journey with a fine-tooth comb. I appreciate all of your constructive criticism. You all took time out of your busy schedules to dedicate your attention to this story.

Brandi Eilert, thank you for the amazing photography work you did to help create a cover page that included an image of an unbelievably strong woman, who fought for not only herself, but for her family and friends as well.

CHAPTER 1: CANCER #1

Famous actress, Patricia Neal once said, "a strong positive mental attitude will create more miracles than any wonder drug."

My mother's attitude during her battle with cancer proved this quote to be true. My mom is a miracle and I was right by her side to witness it all!

In the fall of 2007, my mother went into a gynecologist's office for a routine yearly exam. She had recently moved to Morgantown, West Virginia and had just been given the name of a gynecologist in town that many were fond of and who came highly recommended. My mother scheduled an appointment with Dr. Capelle. She entered the appointment as usual, but left with shocking news. Dr. Capelle had felt an abnormal growth and wanted my mom at the hospital the very next day. I remember waking up early to go to the Monongalia General Hospital, all of us fearful of what they might say. After several tests and being introduced to Dr. Capelle's counterpart, Dr. Ashraf, my mom was scheduled for an immediate hysterectomy and appendectomy. This all took place on Halloween. The irony here is my mother has always hated Halloween. That moment in her life, her hatred towards Halloween grew even stronger. Both doctors confirmed that my mom had stage 2 ovarian cancer. The hysterectomy was only the beginning of my mom's first battle. They successfully removed all of the cancer cells, however, recommended she undergo six months of chemotherapy to ensure none of the "bad" cells had "leaked" out or were left in her body. A new challenge had begun. Not only was my mother facing recovery from a major surgery, but she also was headed into several rounds of intense chemotherapy (chemo).

As she did with the surgery, my mother went into each chemo round with a positive attitude. She walked into every treatment with a smile. She was going once a week to the gynecologist's office where they injected two different chemo drugs into her body. She lost all of her hair and felt as if her identity had disappeared. When she looked into the mirror, she felt as if she was staring at a complete stranger. Her head was bald, she had lost her eyebrows, and her skin was pale. Even around my fiancé, whom she had known for years, she would not be seen without a scarf or wig covering her bald head. Still, she trudged on and kept up an optimistic outlook during each round of chemo. Friends and family took turns weekly to drive her to the doctor. My mom often slept during the actual treatments, so family and/or friends would read magazines or watch the small television in the room, all while waiting patiently for each drip to enter her body. I often remember, on my days of taking her for chemo, looking up at the pump and praying, "Please let this potent drug save my mom's life." The chemo made my mom sick and very tired. It lasted several months and although there were a few good days here and there, the majority of those days my mom was vomiting and wanting to just lie around all day.

Although this lasted over half of a year, looking back now, that period of time seems like a whirlwind that had come and passed before we knew it. I know I did not feel the same way at the time, but I certainly do now. The first cancer was NOTHING compared to what was in store for us.

After the six months of treatment, my mom went into the doctor's office, fingers crossed, for a full-body scan and the results. Had the hysterectomy and chemotherapy been enough to ward off the deadly disease of ovarian cancer? That morning while waiting for the scan, we all felt like throwing up. The doctors told Mom she would have to drink a "dye" of some sort to help get a clear image during her scan. I do not think I would have been able to hold down the dye that morning, having been so nervous myself. Yet again, my mom was a trooper. She sat there slowly sipping the "nasty tasting" liquid prior to being placed in a large tube to see whether or not her six months of hard work had paid off. Would she be healthy again? Dad and I sat for what seemed like eternity waiting for the scan to be over. The worst part was that once it was finished, we simply had to leave the hospital and wait for our results. We still did not have any answers.

Spring, 2008….SUCCESS! Tears of happiness and joy flowed down all of our cheeks the day the phone call came through with the results that once again, my mom was cancer-free! Her everyday life would return to normal. I remember thinking to myself, "my mom is back!" Nothing was going to stop her now. We had to celebrate!

CHAPTER 2: OUR CELEBRATION COMES TO A HALT

Charles Darwin once said, "A man who dares to waste one hour of time has not discovered the value of life."

Every year since I can remember, my family and I have gone to our beach house in Hilton Head, South Carolina for vacation. August of 2008 was no exception. We packed up, my mom, dad, fiancé and I, to hit the beach with a lot to celebrate! (My brother was unable to make the trip due to work, but was going to celebrate in spirit. He felt horrible, but we all knew he would have been there if he could). We could not have been an hour into our drive when my mom said, in a panicked voice, "Oh my god, I forgot 'Chloe'." "Chloe" was the name of her very first wig that we had fallen in love with. It was the perfect cut that looked like my mom's own hair. It was fun shopping for wigs. Each wig had a special name. "Chloe" was our favorite. I knew we were in trouble the minute my mom realized she had left it at home. Her one rule on vacation was that she would not cook. Therefore, we would be dining out! I knew she wasn't quite ready to go "wigless," but she still felt the need to cover her peach fuzz (the little bit of hair she had on her head). We decided as soon as we got there we would hit the shops for a new wig. Several hours later, when we arrived in Hilton Head, we lucked out. We found a cute boutique in one of the shopping centers. For those of you reading this who have never experienced wig shopping, it brings lots of laughs. Something that looks so cute on a manikin can be hideous when you actually put it on your head. The colors of some of the wigs are so far fetched and the cuts are never quite "perfect." After many laughs, from turning my mom into a red head, to having long hair and curls, we found a normal short haircut that would work for the week. Fair warning, wigs are expensive! After our pit stop, we arrived at our house and went straight to the beach. I remember we did not even change; we wanted Mom to see the ocean! We enjoyed the sunset, a yummy dinner out, and were all ready to get some sleep after such a long day of travel.

The next morning we woke up, ate breakfast, put our swimsuits on and headed for the beach. My mom had to be careful with the sun because of the drugs that had been put into her body, but she was thrilled just to have her toes in the sand and know that she was healthy again! We went down every morning and Mom sat under a beach umbrella, soaking in her surroundings and counting her blessings. I remember looking at her and just smiling, so proud of her for putting up such a fight. We were all elated to be at the beach that August. We were relieved to be there and grateful to be on a family vacation after all we had been through. We had talked about it for months. We made a promise to each other that once we got through the ovarian cancer, we would celebrate at the beach.

Our celebration came to a drastic halt! It must have been our third or fourth day into our trip when my fiancé and I were planning an outing to go jet skiing. We had called the marina and made a reservation to go out that afternoon. As I hung up the phone with the jet ski representative, I heard my mom call my name. "Ash, can you come here a minute?" I wandered from my bedroom and hurried across the hall to my parents' room. I found my mom looking at herself in the bathroom mirror, rubbing her neck. There was a lump about the size of a sand dollar, which looked like it was full of some sort of fluid. I had never seen anything like it.

I immediately called Dr. Ashraf in West Virginia, who told us to get my mom to the closest hospital because she had probably developed a blood clot. He wanted her to be given medicine immediately to prevent further clotting and to thin the blood. Upon arriving at the Hilton Head hospital, we were all still semi-calm. In our minds, we would be in and out of there in no time with some medicine, and heading back to the beach the next day. The doctors in the ER observed my mom and started running some blood work. They too believed she just had a blood clot, which could easily be taken care of. However, we were told we would have to wait for the blood work to come back before any further treatment. The doctors at the Hilton Head hospital were astonished when they reviewed the results. My mom's white blood cell count was off the charts! Her numbers were around 96,000 when a typical white blood cell count is 8,000-12,000.

Brian, my mom, dad and I could not believe it. We gave the Hilton Head ER doctors Dr. Ashraf's phone number and had them call West Virginia to consult with him. He too said that it just wasn't possible. He had just seen my mom right before our trip and all of her blood work was normal. The numbers could not have spiked that high in five days. My mom had beat ovarian cancer and had recently had a ton of medical work done proving her to be "cancer-free." All of her numbers had come back in normal range before we left for our trip. Dr. Ashraf continued to refuse the news and told the doctors in Hilton Head to rerun all of the blood work. They ran it and ran it again. The same numbers kept appearing. Looking at the panic on the faces of the ER staff, we knew that something was seriously wrong!

The next thing we knew, Mom was in an ambulance and Dad, Brian and I were following close behind. We drove from the tiny Hilton Head hospital to the closest bigger hospital in Savannah, Georgia. Again, as scared as we all were, Mom calmed us by smiling and waving out of the back windows of her ambulance. The saddest thing was coming off such a high, we had no idea what was ahead of us. To try to pass the time and make the unnerving drive a little better, we were texting back and forth with my mom and continued to laugh and joke. She told us that she was starving. Meanwhile, we were giggling in the car as we ate pretzel rods and Twizzlers. They had been left over from our car ride down to Hilton Head. We would lean over and sneak a bite so Mom couldn't see us. We didn't want to make her feel bad, but we were starving too. Again, everyone kept a positive attitude on our hour-plus drive between Hilton Head, South Carolina and Savannah, Georgia.

Upon arriving at the Savannah hospital, we were checked into a room on the oncology floor. We did not take note as to why we were assigned that floor. In fact, none of us had even noticed the word "oncology" as we got off the elevator. The staff at the Hilton Head hospital had called ahead to set up a room for us. We were going to be there for a while. A very sweet doctor greeted us. She was such a southern belle and brought comfort to our family as she explained they wanted to run more tests and start treatment. Start treatment for what exactly? We still did not know. As with most hospitals, we did a lot of waiting. Mom, Brian, Dad and I were lucky enough to have been given a "suite-like" room that had a pullout couch, recliner, refrigerator, table and chairs. Little did we know that was our home for the next two days. Brian and I were not married yet, so it was uncomfortable sleeping on the pull out couch next to my mom in her hospital bed and my dad in a recliner.

Yet again, Mom trekked on, smiling and joking with all who entered our room. Meanwhile, Dad and I were freaking out and just wanted to know what was wrong. We called back and forth to the doctors in West Virginia, as well as our family members. One morning, the Savannah doctor entered our room with some devastating news. The tests they ran appeared to show that my mom had cancer. Not ovarian this time, but something else. The Savannah hospital wanted to begin treatment that very day. Dad held them off. Somehow, we had to get back home for the long battle ahead. We could not stay in Georgia. My dad had a job to get back to and we did not know how long this whole battle would last. Mom's original doctors were in West Virginia and it would be such a fiasco not being on "home court" for an unknown period of time. We did not plan to make Georgia our home for the next two years, and there was no way we were going to start treatment and then have to move Mom partway through it. We wanted to begin this so-called treatment as soon as possible, but we wanted to do it in West Virginia.

After many phone calls and what seemed like forever, an angel from West Virginia offered to send his private plane to pick up my mom and dad. Not only did this person have a private plane, he arranged to have a medical crew on board in case anything happened. My mom was not allowed to drive the nearly ten hour trip back in the car, but when the hospital got word that she could be flown straight to Morgantown, with a medical staff on board, they gave us permission to go.

That must have been the longest day of my life. Mom and Dad left via charter plane, and Brian and I jumped in the car to drive home and meet them at our third hospital in one week. At least this time, it was our own local hospital back in Morgantown. I remember crying a lot in the car, telling Brian I was scared and asking what was going to happen to my mom? He did what any good fiancé would do and held my hand as he drove and told me everything was going to be all right. He did not share the wheel the entire drive knowing I was unstable and emotionally drained. We did not want anything else on our plates. I remember Dad telling us to take our time and be careful because he couldn't take any more bad news.

We met my parents the next morning. Brian headed home for Maryland to get back to work and Dad and I took Mom to the doctor's office. Here's the kicker. I guess the chemo drugs administered to fight ovarian cancer can lead to leukemia. That is one side effect they never mentioned at the time of treatment months prior. The leukemia, if my mom was going to get it, was not supposed to come for several years. Usually people who beat ovarian cancer remain cancer-free for some time. The potent medicine from the chemo may lead the individual to develop leukemia years after it has been administered. My overachieving mom decided to get leukemia just a few months after her "clean bill of health." She told everyone, again with a smile, "I am overachieving. I am just going to get it over with now." The doctor in West Virginia who confirmed that Mom had leukemia told us that the ovarian cancer was a "walk in the park" compared to what she was about to undergo. He said this would be more like a "biker bar brawl." Dad and I knew we had a long journey ahead.

CHAPTER 3: PREPARED; BUT FOR WHAT?

"Only the unknown frightens men. But once a man has faced the unknown, that terror becomes the known." -Antoine De Saint-Exupery

It's funny in life how things work out. For some odd reason, right before my family vacation, I decided to go into the elementary school where I worked and set up my classroom early. I was the only teacher in the building who had given up her last few days of summer to hang bulletin boards and prepare my classroom. I wanted to go on vacation without having to worry about returning to the grueling task of preparing my classroom for the upcoming year. I had never done this in the past. I always used to wait until the mandatory day for all teachers to return. I never used to give up any extra time in the summer. This year was different. No rhyme or reason, I went in for several days and prepped my classroom. Before I left for Hilton Head my room was completely set up and ready for the first day of school. I was all set!

Everything happens for a reason, huh? Looking back, I know now that there was a reason why I had busted my butt to prepare my classroom before vacation. After talking with family members, specifically, our two closest cousins who had unfortunately lost both of their parents to cancer, we decided that it would be best for me to go on Family Medical Leave and take a year off from teaching. My mom did not want me to do this. However, we did not give her a choice. This is what had to happen. I went into my principal's office, shaking uncontrollably with tears in my eyes, scared of what he may say, or of losing my position. The economy was terrible and I knew if I left my job, there was a very good chance I would not be able to return. The teaching opportunities had just recently become cut throat. Mr. Muhammad was an amazing boss. I remember him calming me down and saying, "Hahn, you know what you have to do." Mr. Muhammad always instilled in his staff that family is the most important thing in life. He told me that I had to be there for my family and not to think twice about my decision. Family comes first and he would do the exact same thing if he were in my shoes. My wonderful team and administration found a long-term substitute to take my place. I will always remember Jennifer Claus who filled in for me during my absence.

That was the last time for an entire year, that I stepped foot into Galway Elementary School. As I walked out of the door, my assistant principal, Mr. Reinke, and my school counselor, Mrs. Curtis, hugged me and told me everything would be all right. Mrs. Curtis handed me a bunch of quotes and methods to use when coping with emotional times. I got into my car and drove straight to West Virginia. The three-hour drive felt like it took me a week. I barely remember focusing on the road, and I couldn't tell you what my speedometer read as I flew through the mountains. My mind was racing. I did not know what the future held for me and I was terrified for my mom. I knew my job was to be by her side every step of the way. I was going to stay upbeat and never let her see me cry. I was going to encourage her every step of the way and not let her give up!

CHAPTER 4: COMMUNICATION

"Outstanding people have one thing in common: an absolute sense of mission." - Zig Ziglar

Dad and I could not take any more phone calls. Our phones were constantly ringing with family and friends calling for updates. We understood they just wanted to know the latest news, but we had to do something different to prevent us from staying on our phones twenty-four hours a day. We had a mission. It was to develop a better means of communication. I decided to send emails out so that everyone heard the same information at the same time. The email list got longer and longer as time passed. Before we knew it, we had friends of friends on the list and Mom's diagnosis was known across the country. Family, friends and even some strangers known as "prayer warriors" were praying for Mom. Below is a copy of the very first email I ever sent.

August 20, 2008
Subject: Momma Hahn

I wanted to send out an email to update everyone on our latest news.

This morning my mom, dad and I went and spoke with one of the doctors from Mon General Hospital. He informed us that Mom has a subtype of ALL (Acute lymphoblastic leukemia) known as MLL (Mixed lineage leukemia: child's form of leukemia). It is a more aggressive form of ALL.

He informed us that he does not specialize in it and we should head over to Ruby Memorial Hospital, which is a teaching hospital by the University right in Morgantown. We checked in room 920 on the Bone

Marrow Unit.

They informed us that the plan (which several doctors consulted on) is to treat it with the following process:

We began tonight with the chemo treatments (approximately 2-4 cycles of chemo, each cycle lasting anywhere between 1-2 weeks). This first one from start to finish will take about 2 weeks. She will then start her second treatment lasting about 4 or 5 days. They hope to then send her home for 2 1/2 weeks. Then the process will continue. (So today, we found out we have checked into the new hospital for 21 days).

The chemo treatments will hopefully lead Mom into remission. Once she is in remission, they will begin a search for a bone marrow match. At this time, they will "type" her and start looking for someone who is a "perfect match." They will check her brother first to see if he is a good candidate (There is only a 25% chance). Anyone and everyone can go and get tested to see if they are a match. They begin testing by taking a blood sample. If not, they will turn to MUD (a mass unrelated donor). Once a match is found, she will undergo a bone marrow transplant.

It will be a long process. The chemo and remission should take us up to the holidays. They are thinking the transplant will be done around the holidays followed by a 6-8 week stay in the hospital.

Please keep her in your thoughts and prayers. Once again, we are staying in room 920 at Ruby Memorial Hospital. They are very cautious up there and do not want any infections. We have to wash thoroughly before entering her room, the door must always be shut, and if she leaves the room, she must wear a mask. They also informed us that there are NO FLOWERS, NO FRUIT, NO CANDIES allowed and any mail sent to mom needs to be opened by someone else. Please ONLY send cards and/or emails. If you want to reach us please call our cells. Thanks :)

Love to all!
Ash

This email resulted in a flood of cards, gifts, emails, phone calls and much more. We had an astounding number of people on our side, all were there for my mom, wanting to help in any way they could. They were praying their hardest for our first medical goal; my mom had to get into remission before anything else could be done. I say medical goal because we also set real-life goals, things that my mom could look forward to.

My mother's number one goal during all of this was to be able to dance at my upcoming wedding. With this news in mind, Brian and I postponed our wedding date by two years. Some might wonder why we didn't get married the very day we heard of my mother's news to ensure that she would be at our wedding. However, I do not believe that is the way anyone should think. Do not live in fear. Of course we wanted my mom at our wedding, but we wanted her there in good health. She would dance at our wedding. We just knew it!

Having two years to plan a wedding is actually very nice. The stresses are a little more spread out and if you book certain venues/vendors by a certain date, they will honor that year's prices, even though they always seem to increase year after year. You are locked in with the prices the day you sign. My mom and I spent hours looking through bridal magazines to pass the time in the hospital. Days when she was down, I pulled out a magazine nonchalantly, which reminded her of her goal. I also held her hand so she could look at my engagement ring.

The first night we left the hospital, Dad and I had a lot to talk about during our drive home. He gave me a pep talk and told me that Mom was a fighter and with all of us praying, she was going to be all right. He told me to be strong and never shed a tear in front of her. He told me it was going to be hard and that I would see my mom very sick. He told me he did not think she was dying and that I should never let that thought cross my mind. Dad also said that we would have to really push Mom to follow all of the doctor's orders.

My dad is a great speaker and has been a collegiate level basketball coach for over twenty-five years. He knows how to persuade people to jump on board with him. He told me that we were in this together and he and I were going to be Mom's anchor. Dad and I set up a game plan that night. He would go into the hospital early in the morning, since he is wide-awake between 5 a.m. and 6 a.m. everyday, and then I would go in around eight o'clock. We would both wait and listen to the "rounds," which are when the doctors come in and share your plan of treatment for the day and whatever else that may lie ahead. After the morning rounds my dad would head off to work and I would stay with Mom. As soon as the workday was over, he would return to be by her side and I would go home for a little while and return later that night. We never wanted to leave her alone. We always wanted someone to be by her side. However, Mom had a different plan. She wanted us to both go home every night to get a good night's rest. My mom was still looking out for the two of us! She is amazing. I doubt I even have to write who won that battle. She did! I would head home in the evenings and make dinner. Dad would come home around 7 p.m. or 8 p.m. after Mom had settled down for the night.

Settling down for the night was such a joke though. Everyone knows they want you to get rest in a hospital, but they sure do make it impossible to get any sleep. They are constantly making noise, and/or poking and prodding, checking in with you, taking your temperature, blood pressure, changing your sheets, asking you to shower, or stopping by with what they call "your next meal." The shift changes don't help because all of the new nurses who come on duty want their own assessment of their patients. The cycle repeats and you may get a few hours of sleep here and there, but there really is nothing quiet about the so-called "quiet hours."

I made sure that Mom got some "quite hours." About once a day, when Mom was about to hit her breaking point, I asked the nurses to give her an hour of uninterrupted rest. Sometimes it meant begging and pleading with the nurses in order to get my way. I would set a one-hour timer and let Mom snooze. I honestly think this was very beneficial for my mom. It also gave her a little something to look forward to.

CHAPTER 5: AUGUST 2008-ARE YOU KIDDING ME?

"There is only one way to get anybody to do anything. And that is by making the other person want to do it." - Dale Carnegie

August 23, 2008
Subject: Momma Hahn Update

Hey guys!

Thank you for all of your kind words, thoughts and prayers. We really appreciate it. Mom and I have been able to read every email sent and Dad, Matt, her and I thank you for all of your support.

It is Saturday 5:10 p.m. and I am sitting here next to Mom. Since the last update, Mom has started her chemo Cycle 1. She has had a total of 7 chemo sessions already, with one dripping as we speak. The doctors are very pleased with how she is responding to the treatments. Her blood cell counts have dropped tremendously from 97,000 almost down to 0. This is their goal of this cycle. On Friday before our "team" of doctors left for the weekend, they told us she looked great on their end. The initial side effects they were concerned about appear to be behind us. :) She has been walking daily, but food is starting to disinterest her. Although as I say that a grilled ham and cheese came in the door and she is loving it :)

That's all for now. I will probably send an email out Monday after we meet with our "team" again.

Love to all...Keep praying!
Ash

PS- Dad gave the medical team a pep talk and they are all treating Mom to beat this and bring home a WIN!!!!! Anyone on our team who did not believe was told to get the hell out!!!

Dad's pep talk was amazing. As I mentioned in the last chapter, my dad is a collegiate basketball coach. Well, I remember that day clearly. When the doctors and nurses came in for their morning rounds, my dad got serious. Coach Hahn at his finest! He pointed at each and every one of them and told them if they didn't think my mom could beat the cancer and if they didn't believe in her, they were to get the hell out! He did not want to see anyone who was not willing to give a 100% effort anywhere near Mom. The looks on their faces were priceless. He ended the conversation by telling them we were all part of a team and there to win. I am not sure whether the doctors and nurses had ever heard such a speech before. He handed each and every member of our team a WVU basketball t-shirt. They left the room and we heard a lot of commotion. I remember thinking, oh man, Dad upset them, they are talking about us right now and this is not good. I thought to myself, they must think we are crazy. Two minutes hadn't even passed by when we had a knock on the door. It was "our team," all wearing their t-shirts, smiling ear to ear. They asked if they could get a picture of all of them with us. They were here to "win!" They were on board. This picture would stay with us forever. Mom, Dad and I joined all of the doctors and nurses in what we could call our 2008 team photograph.

This led us to our first weekend in the hospital. The "A Team" had left and different faces were now taking care of Mom. She continued to do well, but was losing her sense of taste and nothing was appealing to her. She was more exhausted than ever, but again, kept a positive attitude. She did not want to get out of bed to walk, but she did. She did not want to use the nasty tasting mouthwash that prevents mouth sores, but she did. My mom always obeyed EVERYTHING the hospital staff said. She wanted to get out of the hospital as soon as possible. Mom, although she really didn't want to, followed all of their directions. I think she knew if she did not do it on her own, she would have gotten an earful from Dad and I. I, having only been around the hospital for a couple of weeks, was given the name "Nazi Nurse." The doctors, nurses and my very own mother referred to me as this. I would not take "no" for an answer. From forcing her to walk the hallways even when she was dog-tired, to asking the cafeteria to make her something special, if I thought it would help lead to Mom's recovery, it was going to get done. It was my way or the highway. I would, as my dad always taught me, "wear down their resistance with your persistence." I am a "persistent little bugger," but only because I wanted the best for my mom. Not to mention, I wanted to get the hell out of there too. I wanted my mom to be home and have the luxury of sleeping through the night in her own bed!

August 26, 2008
Subject: Momma Hahn Update 3

Good evening! I wanted to touch base with everyone after the weekend and more importantly, after our Monday morning meeting with our team of doctors.

Thank you again for your continuous support. Please keep adding Mom to any prayer lists and/or groups you know of. We believe in the power of prayer and hope these prayers go nationwide :)

Alright...now the details you have been waiting for. On our end, compared to the last email, Mom has had a rough couple of days. She has been a little more nauseas than normal, hasn't had an appetite, and has been knocked on her butt. She struggles to stay awake. You can be talking to her one-minute and the next minute she is sleeping. She is unmotivated to get out of bed and the thought of food makes her stomach churn.

The doctors reassure us that this is ALL absolutely NORMAL. If and when she feels nauseas, they immediately give her some medicine. The pharmacist told us she is so tired because of the chemo all-catching up to her. I will give her credit though; today she walked 2 times with me and attended a relaxation group. She also sat up in a chair for a long period of time. This is important because it keeps her lungs working and helps prevent pneumonia. She ate a small breakfast, did not care for lunch at all, but was able to eat most of her dinner plate.

This morning the doctors told us that they have gotten rid of approximately 95,000 BAD white blood cells. Her count this morning was 500 (a normal person is at 8,000-12,000). This is their goal though. They plan to shoot her down to zero. Since her count is so low, fatigue is expected. It could even get worse the next couple of days. She is also very vulnerable to infection with her count down so low. 80-90% of infections would come from within her own body.

Some good news...her count is down, which is what they want and she will spend a period of time letting her count go back up. She has gone through the first several treatments without getting a fever or any other infections. She is under control and is over the time period when tumerlisis could have happened. (That is something where tumors rupture inside of her and she would have to go under dialysis). So, we are very lucky to have surpassed these side effects.

She was swollen today so they took her down to do an ultrasound on her left side. Good news again....it looked all right and they only saw remnants of the blood clot. :)

Tomorrow they will be doing a chemo treatment through the spine. It will be done in her room and will only take a few minutes. They shoot it into the spine to treat other areas of her body. Most importantly, they want to make sure that there isn't any leukemia hiding in her brain. Other than that, she will have a day of resting.

We are still on track to get out of the hospital on time. We have a post it with a countdown on it. Tonight we tore off day 15, so 14 left to go. We will then be home for a few days before being admitted again for the next chemo cycle. Counting down though!!!! 14 sounds a lot better than our original 21 days!!!! We are rolling! Love to all. Good night.

Ash

PS- Our doctors continue to consult with Dr. DeAngelo from the Dana-Farber Cancer Institute in Boston. He is an expert in treating Acute Lymphoblastic Leukemia patients.

Dad got a tip from a friend that Dr. DeAngelo was a "genius" when it came to Mom's type of cancer. As a coach, my dad always has to make a game plan and this situation was no different. For example, when Maryland played their biggest rival Duke, he would scout the opposing team and come up with a winning plan. Dad would turn to his colleagues who had already beaten their rival and ask them for advice. He used this skill when it came to Mom's medical condition. Dad called Dr. DeAngelo for what his game plan would be if he were Mom's doctor. How would he beat this cancer? The "guru" from the big city of Boston ended up having the exact same plan of attack as Dr. Craig, from a small-town hospital. Dr. Craig was our "A Team" and we knew he was our only chance at a victory.

August 27, 2008
Subject: Hahn Update 4

Thank you! Thank you! Thank you for all of the prayers, cards, letters and warm wishes. It seems to be working! Please understand, that even if I do not respond to each of you individually, we get great joy in reading each email every morning!

So, finally some good news! (Hopefully!!!) The team came in this morning and informed us that Mom was doing great. They are hoping to send her home as an outpatient on Friday night around 8 p.m. Please understand that this will be temporarily and will only happen IF she remains to do a good job the next couple days. She must not come down with a fever or any infections over the next 48 hours.

Our first cycle of chemo is coming to an end and as I said, she did a great job with it. They hope to watch her two more days and send us on our way on Friday after one last 6 p.m. shot of chemo. The plan will be to rest at home and allow her blood cell count to climb back up. During our outpatient time, she will have to get to the hospital every morning by 8 a.m. for a shot and blood work. At anytime, they could admit her again. Also, if any fever spikes we return. So, we will be home, but a little on edge.

The plan is to let her count go up and when it is back to normal 8,000-12,000, they will admit her for the second cycle. At that time, she will be an inpatient again for approximately 4 days. The second chemo cycle should not be as tough on her, but they will keep her to monitor her reactions.

Lastly, they hope that after cycle 2 she may be in remission, however, it could take up to 4 cycles.

Love to all!!!!!!!!!!!!!!!!!!!!!!!!!!!
Ash

When anyone has a loved one in a hospital for any length of time the number one thing you hope and pray for is for the doctor to come in and say that it is time for you to go home. We really did have a countdown going on. We used post it notes that we would tear off daily. It reminded me of the chocolate advent calendar which I used to enjoy counting down the days until Christmas Day. Later in the book, I get more creative with my countdown (please feel free to copy this idea). Somehow visualizing the days disappear really gives you hope. You can actually see an end in sight. We also always teased the doctors and nurses that even though we had our countdown going, they better leave some days on it because we wanted to get out of there early. At times, we even tended to get a little pushy with them.

I remember day after day anxiously awaiting the word "home" to come out of the doctor's mouth. However, the first time it happened I was filled with mixed emotions. Could I take care of my mom at home? Was she going to be really sick? What if we had to turn around and go right back? All I could do was follow the doctor's orders on our discharge papers. I prayed for an uneventful period of time when my mom could rest and feel better in the comfort of her own house.

August 30, 2008
Subject: Hahn Update 5

Sitting here next to Mom.......on the COUCH in our man room at home!!!! WOOHOO!!!!!!!!!!
We were released today at 7 p.m. as an outpatient. However, we are still on edge because any fever, chill, infection, etc. can land us back in the hospital. The plan is to stay out until her white blood cell count goes back up. She is at 200 right now. We will have Saturday off completely (other than the millions of pills we have to give her), and will have to go in Sunday morning at 8 for blood work and shots. If all remains looking good, we will follow that routine for several days. In at 8 am and home the rest of the day and night.

Once the count is up, we will check back in for 4 or 5 days to complete cycle 2. Cycle 2 will be all new drugs and they will watch her closely to see how she reacts. However, they did say that cycle 2 tends to be a little better than cycle 1.

Hopefully you will not hear from me for several days as we soak up our time at home. Matt has been here since Thursday and will return to Vermont on Monday. We will miss him, but I know my mom has been so thankful that her mama's boy made it in before the crazy season.

Love to all.
Ash

PS-Her appetite is back. She requested homemade potpie, linguini, and burnt hotdogs, along with every kind of fruit and dessert you could imagine.

It is hard to imagine that as a daughter you would ever have to take care of your mother. I was 25 years old and forced to grow up fast. As my cousins put it, "my mom's illness was the best thing that ever happened to my fiancé." I was forced to learn how to cook, clean and manage a house. Dad and I took turns making dinner, doing the laundry, etc. Mom, when well enough, taught me every single recipe she knew. I clearly remember her saying, "add a pinch of salt." I would literally take the salt and a measuring spoon over to her and tell her to show me her pinch. I would then measure it out so I could write down the exact amount. Anyone who has ever seen a recipe of mine knows how dummied down it has to be. They start with the very basics such as preheat oven, while water boils do such and such. My mother is an amazing cook and if I was going to be cooking for her for a year, I wanted her to love my cooking as much as I loved hers. Every recipe in my repertoire came from her!

My mom could not get enough fruits and desserts. I asked the doctors why she had been experiencing those cravings. They said that the drugs might have affected her sense of taste, therefore, the strength of the sweetness in the fruits and desserts were appealing to her. It was wonderful to see her craving food again. Unfortunately, Dad and I were packing on the pounds because we could not pass on the yummy desserts we were sharing with her.

CHAPTER 6: SEPTEMBER 2008- CANCER #2 BATTLE CONTINUES

"When you're going through hell, keep going." - Winston Churchill

September 4, 2008
Subject: Hahn Update-6

Hey folks. I haven't sent out an update since Friday, so I thought I would check in. We are enjoying our time at home. Below are some short daily updates:

Friday-Got released as an outpatient in the evening. Loved hanging out on the couch/her own bed and the fact that the family was home all-together including Matt :) Did not sleep very well b/c she kept waking up waiting for a nurse or someone to be in her face.

Saturday- A really nice day. We did not have to go in at all, so we enjoyed spending time as a family watching the WVU football game. Matt was surprisingly a huge help with drinks, cleaning up, giving Mom pills, etc.

Sunday-We had to check into the hospital for a few hours. They drew blood, checked on her vitals, and informed us her count is at 100. She will be extremely tired. When we got home, we enjoyed potpie dinner and long naps.

Monday- Went in again at 8 am. Informed she would need a bag of platelets and some bags of fluids. Longer stay in the hospital from about 8-1. Checked back out and had to say goodbye to Matt. (That sucked!!!!)

Count still at 100.

Tuesday- Not as good as the weekend. Chemo started catching up with her. She had to stay for a few hours of liquids and extra potassium. Extremely tired and not as perky as over the weekend. Count still at 100.

Wednesday-By far the worst day yet. Went in at 8 am. She was told her blood pressure was very low and she was dehydrated. They also wanted to perform the second spinal tap. We were at the hospital from 8 am until about 2:00. She was extremely tired, could not keep her eyes open for more than two minutes and completely drugged from the procedure and other nausea medicine, etc. I had to call my dad at work to meet me at the house to help her walk. (Picture staggering drunken sailor walk). She slept ALL day and ALL night. She could not keep her eyes open. However, she nailed the second spinal treatment!!! :)

BUT.....along with our not so good day, came some good news!!!

1.   Her count is where they like it...she will probably remain this low for about a week before her numbers shoot back up. They give her daily shots when we visit that are supposed to help her count climb up.

2.   On Monday, they want us to meet with Dr. Craig (the head of the bone marrow unit) at the Cancer Center (which is connected to the hospital) to find out our plan of action. At this time, they may even check to see if she is in remission. Keep those prayers rolling. They are still really impressed with her reaction to cycle one and how well she is doing at home (must be Dad, Matt, and my awesome work). No matter what, remission or not, we will still go through with cycle 2. Once her counts are up, we will check into the hospital for up to a week to complete that cycle.

3.   Instead of needing 16 spinal treatments, they will be performing 8. This is great news. Each one will become easier and easier. Not to mention we are already done with 2!!!! :) We continue to do these as precautionary measures to ensure that there isn't any leukemia hiding out in her brain. (Oh, and the first treatment showed NO SIGNS of cancer in the brain).

Lastly, today:

Thursday- We were in and out of the hospital. Checked in at 8, home by 11:30. Everything looked good again other than a little dehydration. They pumped 2 hours of fluid into her. She was able to stay awake most of the morning and has a little more energy today (not much). I just got her into bed for a nap. She loves to sleep right now and fatigue is absolutely normal with her count where it is.

She did begin to lose her hair today though, so the nurses helped by cutting it while we were there. That way, she would not need to watch it happen and make a mess. It is so difficult to see clumps of hair on your pillow or come out in the shower. She has a clean shaven cut, and handled it much better than the first go around with ovarian cancer. I guess knowing it comes back and seeing how fast she grew that hair really helped!

Sorry this was so long. Thanks again for all of your kind words. Keep praying hard!!! Love to all.

Ash

September 8, 2008
Subject: Mom Update: Sept 8

Hey everyone! Fact of life: Most people love the weekends and dread Monday mornings. NOT US!!!! This weekend we were feeling just the opposite!!!

Saturday and Sunday were not very good days for my mom. Saturday she went in for her normal blood work and shots at 8 am. Her blood pressure dropped waaaayyyy low and she ended up fainting in the hospital. She needed two bags of blood and more fluids. They took blood cultures and watched her. After 7 hours of treatments they let her go home.

Sunday she woke up to go in at 8 a.m. Since she had all of that work on Saturday, they kept us there for a short amount of time, informed us her blood count was at 22,000, which meant the shots had been working, and sent us home for the day. UNFORTUNATELY, we were not even home an hour when the phone rang. The blood cultures from Saturday came back and they found bacteria in it. They rushed us back into the hospital for an antibiotic and a few days of monitoring her.

We couldn't wait for Monday morning to talk to our dream team and see what was up.

TODAY (Monday) brought us great news!!!! Our dream team was back and they sat down with us. The resident who had been on duty on Sunday was being extremely cautious when he heard of the bacteria. He gave her the right antibiotics and was smart to watch her for 24 hours. BUT, we found out that we would be released today!!!! As of this morning, her blood work showed a normal red blood cell count, a normal platelet count, and her white blood cells are at 11,000. This is absolutely on track. Anybody who is not sick has a count of 8,000-12,000. She is looking good! They actually called her normal :)

They continued to inform us that the bacteria was probably nothing to worry about (with the antibiotic in her system) and that with her white blood cell count at a normal number, she should be able to fight anything else off by herself. We have been sent home for 2 1/2 full days. We do not even need to go in for a shot or any blood work all day Tuesday and Wednesday (this is great since those are my dad's two days on the road recruiting). We will finally try again to meet with the head of the bone marrow unit on Thursday at 3:00 to discuss our next plan of action.

Mom is doing very well. They usually do not let people go home after cycle one. They told us she cruised through it and that is why she has had some days at home. We are hoping to find out if she has made it to remission on Thursday. This would be great, however, she will still probably need 4 full cycles of this chemo before the transplant. We will know a lot more on Thursday.

It's obvious that our prayer network has been working. The prayers have been answered through cycle one; please continue to pray throughout the next chemo rounds and several months ahead!!!

Cards are still welcomed and very appreciated. It is best to send them to the house. (Address went here). I will send out an email Thursday evening.

Love to all!!!
Ash

After all Mom had already been through, I could not believe that only a month had passed. It was going to be a long road. From the time we found out Mom had leukemia, until the first round of chemo was over, felt like forever. Unfortunately, our challenges had only just begun. I tried to spread out the emails, but there was just too much to share with friends and family. Typing the emails was like keeping a diary. It was nice to be able to write everything down and at the same time it helped me relieve some stress. I thought by sending constant emails to everyone, the phone would stay a little quieter, but calls constantly poured in. I was exhausted, but the emails gave me support and I knew as long as the updates kept flowing, the prayers would be on our side.

September 11, 2008
Subject: Hahn update Sept 11

Hey guys!

We were overwhelmed with information today after meeting with the head of the bone marrow unit. I will do my best to relay all of the information below. Bear with me if some of my medical terms are spelled wrong or don't make sense. I am forwarding the information the best I can. I apologize for the length of this email, but we learned A LOT today.

I will begin by sharing some good news. Mom did a great job with cycle one and her count has fully recovered. We have enjoyed a few days at home without any shots or IV's. We even got to enjoy lunch out on a dock by a lake and a trip to Target :) It was so nice to do a few "normal" things. She looks great right now and has even been wearing makeup and jewelry!

Next steps:
So the plan is to go in tomorrow, Friday, to have a bone marrow test to see how everything is going. It is an outpatient procedure and will be done at the cancer center. While she is there, the doctor will remove her triple lumen (the port they have in right now). He informed us the triple lumen is not the best line to have. It sounds as if he is able to remove it by pulling it out.

He has planned for her to go into the hospital on Monday to get a new "pick line" put in. (Similar to a port-an easy way to inject meds without always having to poke her veins). Then either Monday or Tuesday start cycle 2 of chemo.

Ok...so the info overload:

-Dr. Craig believes the leukemia was caused by the chemo that was used to treat her ovarian cancer.

-There are two major steps to treat this. First is the chemo, second the transplant. The transplant is a huge amount of effort, a lot of work and very risky. Mom's blood producing system will be replaced with someone else's and her immune system will also be replaced in order to protect her from infection and also help fight and keep the leukemia away.

-There is a 40% long-term survival rate. She must get into remission before getting the transplant. The transplant is done like a blood transfusion in which she would get a bag and drip it through her IV.

-They will send Mom's brother a kit to start the process of checking to see if he is a match. There is only a 25% chance he will be a match. PLEASE PRAY FOR THIS. It would be ideal. Otherwise, they will begin searching the National Bone Marrow Donor Program. It could take months to find an unrelated donor. You cannot specifically go get tested for Mom. You would have to become part of the bone marrow donor program. If my uncle is a match, he will come here, if the match is someone nationwide or even worldwide, the cells would be flown here.

Our plan includes a primary and secondary treatment. The primary treatment is an aggressive therapy where she will be an inpatient for about a week and then outpatient as her cells recover (just like this first cycle):
-4 cycles of chemo, 1 down, and the 4th starting around early November
-a total of 8 spinal taps -to protect the brain (2 of which she has already had)
Secondary treatment-1 full month in the hospital:
-Prep regimen, which is a week of chemo with higher doses
-Transplant- Transfusion lasts about 2 hours, she is given a new blood system, cells will divide and start working finding their way into their new home (her body)
-Recovery
The cells will recover in 10-20 days, however, recovery lasts a lifetime. The cells need to mature and protect her for a lifetime.

***There are 3 major problems that can occur with the transplant.
-Graft vs. host disease: This is when the new immune system attacks you. There are medicines on board to prevent it. However, 50-60% of people have a mild case of this disease, which is treatable, but then there is a 15-20% chance of severe which is hard to fight.
-Relapse of leukemia (10-15%)
-Infections

This is a long process that we are only a month into. It is most important that we do not lose your prayers along the way. We need everyone's support throughout the next 3 cycles, 6 spinal taps remaining, search for a donor, transplant and recovery! Don't forget us as time goes by!!!

I will end by saying...we love our head doctor and he told Mom she should be able to dance at my wedding in two years. He said it is most important to not take it day by day, but to look at the final goal.

Love to all,
-Ash

September 11, 2008 was the day I decided that I loved our head doctor. Love is an understatement. Dr. Craig is the most amazing doctor anyone could dream of having treat a loved one. He is down to earth, honest, and gives everyone who speaks to him a sense of security. He takes time with his patients and really makes them feel comfortable. It is reassuring knowing he is the one responsible for caring for your loved ones. He really knows what he is doing and has the gentlest tone to his demeanor. Little did I know, that was the beginning of an incredible bond between Dr Craig and myself. To this day, two years later, we have kept in touch. I love that when Mom goes back in for check ups with Dr. Craig, he asks her how the "boss" is doing. He is not asking about how my mom or my dad are doing. He is asking about me. I'm "the boss!"

Dr. Michael Craig, the coach of "our team"

There was definitely a lot of information handed to us on that day. They did a great job of explaining everything, but at the same time, scared the living daylights out of us. The scary side effects were definitely not something we wanted to hear. Even with all of the great news that day, the bad parts were what stuck with us. Our minds constantly wondered and we tried to replay the doctor's words over and over again in our minds to try to digest the new information.

I suggest when you go into a doctor's office that you have a pen and paper available to jot down notes. Whenever we met with the doctors or nurses I would write everything down. Sometimes when you hear something negative, it is all you hone in on and you might miss other information. By writing it all down, you are able to revisit the information provided as well as process it and refer to it in case you have any questions.

One amazing thing my mom did in regard to the side effects of her treatment was to simply "forget about them." She often said, "don't tell me what can happen or it will happen to me. If I don't know about it, then it won't happen." It was true. She did not want to know what any of the side effects were. She preferred to have the doctors talk privately with my dad and I. If she heard that she might feel nauseas, then she did, but if those words were never mentioned to her, she would have felt fine. I guess it was a mind game and maybe a little hypochondriac syndrome. This was how she dealt with those things, and I must say, it really did help. She avoided several of the possible side effects.

September 15, 2008
Subject: Hahn Update Sept 15

Just a real short update...Mom checked back into the hospital this morning. She got a picc line put in today. It was not as bad as she thought it would be. Very quick process. They've started her on fluids. She will begin cycle 2 of chemo tomorrow. They hope to have us checking out as an outpatient on Friday or Saturday to recover her counts at home again!
Love to all
Ash

September 18, 2008
Subject: Hahn update Sept 18

Keep praying! Please keep praying!
Prayers are being answered!!!
Mom has made it to remission!!!!! Woohoo!!!!! :)

She had a bone marrow test on Friday and we were given the good news today. After starting at 100,000 bad cells, they were shocked that she went into remission after one round. They checked three different things; premature cells, chromosome 11 and something else and everything came back negative. What an overachiever!!!!! She is doing awesome!!!!

Update:

We have been back in the hospital since Monday receiving cycle 2 of chemo. She has been doing well with it and we have been cleared to go home Friday to recover pending no complications. It appears we will be home for approximately two weeks as her count drops and recovers. I will be giving her daily shots and other meds and we will visit the cancer center two times a week during that time.

Love to all! BIG HUGS! Don't forget this is a long process, but step one is done!!!

Ash

Remission. Ahhhh....a sigh of relief. We did it! Our first medical goal. Check! Thumbs up to Mom. What a trooper! That word brought tears to our eyes. We were that much closer to Mom being able to have a transplant. Not to mention, she was getting her life back on track and would soon be cancer-free. Little did we know at that time, we were still five months away from her transplant.

September 25, 2008
Subject: Hahn update Sept. 25

Hey everyone! Just a little update. We have been home since last Friday. We went in for labs and a doctor visit today. The labs showed a white blood cell count of 100, very low, with her platelets dropping as well. All normal and what they want.

She will continue to drop (maybe even down to zero). I give her two shots daily to help her counts recover. She also takes daily pills to help fight infections.

We will return to the cancer center on Monday for a blood transfusion and some platelets...it is a 2 1/2 hour drip into her PICC line. We will then go home. We are scheduled to gets labs every Monday and labs/doctor visits every Thursday for the next two weeks.

They think she will be an outpatient for two more weeks and are looking to start cycle 3 sometime between October 10-13. The next round will be back to cycle one and will include a few spinal taps. Again, we will plan to be in the hospital 5 days, followed by a few weeks at home.

Lastly, they fed-exed a kit to my mom's brother, Uncle Tim, today. He will be tested to see if he is a match. We will get the results hopefully by October 15th. Please pray for a match!

Love to all
Ash

Side story: My uncle is so funny. He was willing to be tested, but acted like such a baby when he talked to me on the phone about the process. If he was a match, he wanted to know, would it hurt him and who would take care of him? What a typical male. He was practically begging for sympathy even though he had yet to be tested. Anyway, when his test package arrived, my uncle went straight down the street to get his marrow tested. (The initial screening to become a donor is a cheek swab with a q-tip. I did it and it was easy. My uncle's process was a bit more involved because of his relationship to Mom. Due to the fact that Mom and Uncle Tim are siblings, he was able to bypass the initial screening process). The first lady he spoke with at the lab could not even find the necessary paperwork to complete the testing. She was in the process of informing my uncle that she had never administered the test and before she could even finish her sentence, a large woman came stomping in from behind and said, "I don't care what the hell we have to do." The new, larger woman had taken over for the initial lady who was unsure about the whole process. She went on and drew my uncle's blood, wrapped it securely and told him, "Honey, take this right down the road and mail it yourself." I am sure he was in some sort of violation when he sent his blood through the mail, however, he did not waste any time. He immediately mailed his kit to the National Marrow Donor Program. Was Uncle Tim a match?

Back to my story: Imagine having to give your mother two shots daily. Wow. Who knew a kindergarten teacher could also be a nurse? I hated every morning asking my mom to roll her sleeve up so I could pinch her skin and stick her with a needle. The worst part was that the drug burned if it was not administered slowly. Each shot felt like an eternity. She told me towards the end that I was better at giving her shots than some of the nurses at the hospital. That made me feel like I was doing a good job. My mom knew she had to reassure me since every time I gave her a shot, I felt nauseous. The shots really helped Mom's counts climb, so I always had to remind myself that every shot would mean we were a little closer to Mom's recovery.

CHAPTER 7: OCTOBER 2008- MOM HATES OCTOBER

"I didn't find my friends; the good Lord gave them to me." –Ralph Waldo Emerson

October 6, 2008
Subject: Hahn Update Oct. 6

Hey everyone...haven't heard from me in awhile because things have been going well. Mom has recovered her counts again; therefore, her reward is to check back in for round 3 and one more spinal tap. She will be admitted to the hospital on Wednesday. The chemo treatment will last several days and we hope to be released on Sunday or Monday. (Again, at home, her count will drop down low and with daily shots and medicine should fully recover in about 2 weeks).

Also, Uncle Tim has been tested and we will find out if he is a match by October 15th.

Please keep this in your prayers as well as a smooth 3rd cycle.

Hugs
Ash

PS- Matt and his girlfriend will be visiting this weekend. We look forward to seeing him and meeting her. Also, my best friend Lisa is running a marathon in honor of my mom on Saturday. She raised over $3000 for leukemia research.

In and out of the hospital became the norm. The ninth floor of Ruby Memorial Hospital was our second home. We became friends with the doctors, nurses and other families up there. Everyone was in the same boat. One family we became particularly close to was the Riley family. Aaron was a young man, 21 years old, who had been diagnosed with leukemia. His family was so caring and loving, and his sister was even a nurse at the cancer center. We should have known our families would be close to one another when we found out Mom and Aaron shared the same birthday. On July 14th two special people were born. Many loved Aaron and his room was always full of visitors. I would often stop by when Mom was napping, because his room had it all. He always had friends or family there. He set up videogames, watched DVDs, played darts from his hospital bed, dressed up in funny wigs and simply entertained himself and others with his bubbly personality. Dad became close with Aaron and often went in for early morning visits. He would sit right on Aaron's bedside and give him pep talks. Unfortunately, Aaron did not beat his battle with cancer. He never seemed to catch a break and often faced infections and other complications. Aaron is now up in heaven and is living his life cancer-free. His story touched us, and Mom still sees Abby, his sister, every time she goes to the cancer center.

Abby always hugs Mom and says how great she looks. She could have easily turned her back after losing her brother to cancer and resent the fact that Mom was doing well. However, Abby continues to support Mom. It just shows you what amazing people Abby and her family are. We couldn't be more pleased to have someone like her caring for Mom.

Along with Aaron and his family, I personally became friends with some of the nurses on the ninth floor. Many of them were around my age and they knew I did not have many friends in Morgantown, since my home was in Maryland. Kristen was one of the nurses with whom I have stayed in touch with. She and I went out for dinner and drinks a couple of times. Her husband also worked in the hospital and our family was very fond of the both of them. Another nurse I loved was Sam. Sam and I had a lot of inside jokes. I will never forget one day walking out into the hall saying, "Mmm Sam, it smells so good, like Chinese food." (I was always planning my next meal, and still do). She started laughing hysterically. I said, "What? Are you craving it too? I will go get us some." At that point, she looked at me with disgust and said, "Ashley, I don't know why you think it smells good, that is a patient you smell who just had massive diarrhea and I cleaned it up." I was disgusted. Needless to say, I did not order Chinese food that day, and that became a daily joke between Sam and I. To this day, I still laugh about my "poopy craving!"

October 13, 2008
Subject: Hahn Update Oct 13

Just wanted to let everyone know we were discharged today. Mom had spent 5 days in the hospital completing cycle 3 along with a spinal tap. She did pretty well other then some weight gain and swollen arms/legs. They checked for blood clots to be safe, but tests came back negative. She has retained so much water and they ensure us it will go down at home since she is no longer hooked up to fluids and will be able to move around a lot more than when she is in the hospital.

Next Monday she will need to go to the cancer center as an outpatient for one more dose of chemo and another spinal tap. Other than that we will follow the same routine we have in the past. She will continue taking meds at home and will be given daily shots until her white blood cell count drops to nothing and recover again. We will continue to go to the cancer center twice a week for labs. In about three weeks, we will check back in for the final round of chemo :)

Also, I finally had the chance to download some pictures, so attached are the following:
-A picture of our team of doctors from cycle 1. (Dad gave them all shirts. They left our room, then surprised us by immediately putting them on and asked for a picture with Mom)---This is found above in the book.
-A picture of one of my best friends running a marathon in honor of my mom. She raised over $3000 for the leukemia foundation----This can be found below.
-A picture of the shirt everyone had on to go cheer for her.----This can be found below.

Hope you enjoy! Love to all.
Ash

PS- Matt's visit was great. We had a really nice time AND his girlfriend fit right in with the fam. She survived the weekend, even with my dad teasing her...lol :)

-Lisa running on behalf of my mother.

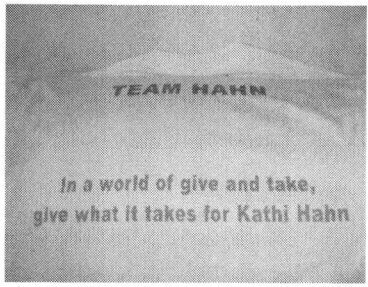

-The back of the t-shirts she had made.

At this point in my book, I would like to put in a plug for the National Bone Marrow Donor Program. Please, please, please sign up to be a donor. Everyone has it wrong. When people think bone marrow donor, they automatically think pain. There is nothing to it anymore. A simple cheek swab is all you need to join the registry and possibly save a life, just as someone did for my mom :). Since all of this, I have signed up and really hope one day I will be called to save another mother, just like my own. (Please note in the following email it says the kit costs $55. However, I got my kit in the mail for free).

October 16, 2008
Subject: Hahn Update October 16-We need your help!

Attention all strapping young men and anyone who knows one. We need you to sign onto the National Marrow Donor Program and join. http://www.marrow.org

We received some unfortunate news today that my Uncle Tim is NOT a match to mom. We are extremely bummed. Our bone marrow coordinator told us that they would now begin a worldwide search for shockingly....a young, healthy male. They would be the next best match for Mom! It costs $55 for a kit to be tested and it is mailed directly to you. The test is a simple cheek swab...the most painful thing is the cost, so just bite it and get this done. If you don't save my mom's life, you could save someone else's.

Some other info we received today:

1. The worldwide search could take months. If it takes too long, they will add an additional chemo cycle to our plan to ensure the leukemia doesn't return.

2. For the transplant, Mom will be an inpatient for 4-6 weeks. Once she is discharged she will then be an outpatient for 2 months and will need care 24hrs a day/7 days a week. My job :) I will have to take a class and pass a test before she is released....oh boy, more pressure...lol

3. When she checks in for the transplant she will undergo a week of high dose, brand new chemo to prepare her body for someone else's cells. She will then receive the transplant followed by 10-14 days of an extremely low count in which she will feel the worst she has ever felt. Lastly, there will be a recovery period until they feel she is ready to be on her own.

4. There are some extremely dangerous side effects with this procedure including something known as graft vs. host disease in which her body rejects the new cells.

***We REALLY need your prayers to continue!!!!!!! Thanks to everyone who goes and gets tested. Love you all......We can do this!!!!! We are a strong, faithful family who will never stop fighting!!!

Ash

It is hard to understand the ups and downs of cancer and the chemo rounds. One minute the patient can be sick as a dog and the next they can feel like they are absolutely healthy and wonder if they even have cancer. It is amazing week-to-week, even day-to-day, you never know what to expect. On Mom's "good days," we would run around and set up some things for the wedding such as flowers, the cake, etc. It was nice to have this goal and constant reminder of one reason why Mom should keep fighting.

October 27, 2008
Subject: Hahn update Oct. 27-good news

Hey everyone! I am writing a happy email today :) Thank you to EVERYONE who has been tested or have signed up to be tested. Please, please continue to be tested AND tell everyone you know how easy it is and to sign up!!! Even if we were to find a match, we need you because it could fall through!!!!

Now for the good news.
Mom was approved for a grant, which will cover all tests for potential matches. The process costs $2000 a person and can add up really quickly. So, Mom and Dad are very relieved and I am thrilled they won't need to touch my wedding fund :) LOL...j/k

Ready for the great news:
They ran a preliminary screen and found a few potential matches. One is a possible 12/12 match and we have two other people who are potential 11/12 matches, which is fine as well. They will be contacted for urgent testing to keep this ball rolling. We will hear back in 4 weeks. IF this works, then Mom will remain on schedule for an X-Mas transplant. This would mean NO EXTRA chemo....SO keep praying for this match!!!

We check back in the hospital Thursday for our last round of chemo and two more spinal taps.

Love to all,
Ash

PS-Last Thursday I took Mom to labs and her numbers looked good, so we jumped in the car for a surprise visit to Aunt Barbara in Salisbury. For those of you who don't know, she is Mom's "cancer cousin" who is also facing her second cancer. She successfully had brain surgery and it was perfect timing. The ladies sat in bed all weekend and even made it out for lunch. It was a wonderful visit!!!

My mom's cousin, Aunt Barbara, was a wonderful woman who gave so much in her life. She was a true philanthropist. Her daughters, my cousins, were the only way I got through all of this. They were the ones that told me I had to leave my job, move to West Virginia and be by my mom's side. Angie and Julie had been through the cancer battle with their father at a young age, and then their mother. They were the ones who supported me when I was scared, tired, and ready to give up. They were the sisters I never had. Aunt Barbara and Mom pushed each other and told one another they would be healthy again one day. Aunt Barbara and Mom joked about how they were outdoing and one-upping one another with each medical challenge. Again, laughter and joking is one way to handle a tough situation.

As I write this, I am reminded of a story. Since my uncle had passed away several years before, my aunt decided to start dating again. The man she began seeing was very special to my aunt. His name was Mr. Draper and he had much shorter hair, practically shaved. Well, kids do say the darndest things. One morning my mom was showering and getting ready. She had hung her wig on the bedpost as she got herself dressed. One of Aunt Barbara's grandkids ran into the bedroom and saw my mother's wig hanging there. Unsure of what it was at a young age, he ran into where my aunt was laying in bed, and wide-eyed as if he had seen a ghost, yelled, "Grammy, Mr. Draper's hair fell off and is hanging on the bed." We all laughed hysterically and every time the little boy went by the room where my mom was staying, he peaked in shyly, looking for the hair that was never to be seen again.

Aunt Barbara, unfortunately, passed away. It was a sad time for all. Although one might think Mom would have given up after seeing this, she did not. Instead, Mom decided that she was going to put up an even BIGGER fight. She was not going to let this horrible "C" word get the best of her. She wanted to be there for Aunt Barbara's daughters and grandchildren. Between Angie and Julie, Aunt Barbara had seven grandchildren, who meant the world to her. I knew I wanted all seven in my wedding. Aunt Barbara left me money to help my parents pay for the wedding. She knew how even with insurance, the medical bills were adding up. Laying on her deathbed, Aunt Barbara wrote in shaky handwriting, a note to her daughters that said, "Ashley's Wedding." As sick as she was, she still continued to give. Mom was going to be sure to dance at my wedding. I was so sad my aunt wouldn't be there. I knew she would be watching from up above and I knew she was once again reunited with her husband whom she had lost years before, both living cancer-free in heaven.

CHAPTER 8: NOVEMBER 2008- THANKSGIVING IN VEGAS

"Perhaps it takes a purer faith to praise God for unrealized blessings than for those we once enjoyed or those we enjoy now." ~A.W. Tozer

November 4, 2008
Subject: Quick Hahn update

After a bit of delay due to a low platelet count, Mom checked into the hospital today, Tuesday for round 4 (hope to be out by Saturday). Good news though, she is on schedule and we may be able to go to Vegas with Dad's basketball team for Thanksgiving. We booked our flights with insurance hoping to have a big hurrah before the 100-day check in for the transplant!

Love to all,
Ash

It felt so great to book a flight and to feel like we were a normal family again. One of the perks of having a dad as a basketball coach is that we get to travel to different locations for tournaments. West Virginia always books a November tournament and Mom and I were not going to miss it if she was well enough to go. Vegas baby! We thought for sure that we deserved a little vacation before the dreaded transplant and our 100-day stay at our other resort, aka Ruby Memorial.

Dad has become friends with famous sports psychologist, Dr. Jerry Lynch. During this chapter of my dad's life, he decided to turn to his friend for some support and guidance for Mom. Dr. Lynch is known for teaching, "mental toughness for competitive peak performance in sports, business, and life." He believes in the "way of champions." My mother is a champion! She is a bigger winner than any athlete or superstar out there. On November 12, Dr. Lynch sent Dad an email to forward to Mom.

Hi Kathy...been thinking of you lately. Billy
called and told me about your situation. There seems to be no words that
could adequately express my feelings at this time and I imagine you feel the
same way. Life tends to be absurd at times yet I trust everything has a purpose even if we can't see it at the time. I am visualizing, praying and somehow I know that it will all work out just fine. I invite you to call me anytime (or email as well) to talk about this. Please don't hesitate.
(---)_ _ _ - _ _ _ _ (his number was here)
Sending you much Chi and love today...
Warmest regards, Jerry Lynch

I remember it took her some time, but she called him and felt a lot better after they spoke. Their conversation was private, but my mom had an even better attitude after their phone call. Hard to believe she could be even more upbeat and positive than she had been during that time period, but the 5-minute phone call boosted her spirits even more!

November 24, 2008
Subject: Hahn Update Nov 24

Vegas Baby, here we come!!!!!!!!!!!!!! Sorry I haven't emailed in awhile; we just were taking the time to recover from the fourth cycle. Good news today. Mom was approved to go to Vegas for Dad's basketball tournament over Thanksgiving!!! We went to labs today and she had good numbers. They gave her two bags of blood to ensure she was all pumped up for the trip!!! She even has been approved to drink a few drinks each day! Woohoo!!!! This will be such a fun trip..somehow slots manage to take everything off your mind. I hope she hits big...she deserves it!

As for a medical update....two of our four potential donors dropped out of the bank. HOWEVER.....2 are hanging on. One potential match has already scheduled their appointment and has completed their further testing. We will have their results in approximately 10 days. The other potential match has an appointment scheduled for December 3rd for further testing. This is a very good sign. I asked the doctor if our potential 12 for 12 match was still in the running and he said, "Yes, they are still around." I hope it is the one who has already been tested.

A bit of "ugh" news. Because we are now on the donor's schedule, the transplant probably will not take place until January or February. Therefore, Mom will have to continue the chemo cycles. We will return from Vegas and she will check into the hospital for round 5. Everything happens for a reason. She will then be able to enjoy Christmas at home as her counts recover again. The doc ensured us that the chemo is just as important as the transplant, so it is fine to continue treatments while waiting for the transplant.

That is all for now. Hope everyone has a HAPPY THANKSGIVING!!!! We will be thinking of you from the Mirage in Vegas, hopefully, hitting the jackpot. We are soooo pumped!!!!!

Love to all!!!
Ash

CHAPTER 9: DECEMBER 2008- THE HOLIDAYS

"I wish we could put up some of the Christmas spirit in jars and open a jar of it every month." *-Harlan Miller*

Mom in her famous "chloe" wig pictured with Dad

December 1, 2008

Subject: Hahn update Dec 1

Well folks....we did it!!! We went to Vegas and returned without any problems. Mom and I especially had an awesome time. We gambled from morning until night, went to two basketball games, saw Jersey Boys and had a wonderful Thanksgiving dinner with the team. We REALLY needed this time away from the grind here. It was nice to be having fun and not worrying about a thing other than how much we were "depositing" at each casino...lol :)

I did have some luck!!! My first night there I hit for $1000!!!! It paid for my trip, some meals, and a fun night out with the girls on the town.

Dad was super busy. His team beat Iowa on Friday and went to the championship game against Kentucky on Saturday. Unfortunately, his team lost. They looked like poop and I could have done a much better job on the court than any one of his guys that night. Mom and I made TV as we sat on the court under the basket. Dad is hustling now to prepare for Mississippi, which he plays on Wednesday.

Mom was a trooper who could not be stopped. She loved it!!!! We will have one week off before heading in for round 5 of chemo. We are scheduled to check into the hospital on Tuesday the 9th.

Love to all,
Ash

The Vegas trip was amazing. Just to feel "normal" again. Thanksgiving dinner with Mom and Dad was a blessing. We had a lot to be thankful for already. For those of you who know Mom, she loves to play slots. There were nights when I was exhausted and she was still wired to keep on going. This is what I dreamed of the last few months, my mom was back.

One of the side effects from all of Mom's treatments was huge, swollen ankles! The longer she was on her feet, the worst they got. Some days it looked like her ankles were as big as those of an elephant. After an entire day of basketball games and slots, Mom's ankles were huge. A case of what we called at the time, "elephant-titis." Dad had his only night off in Vegas and asked me if I wanted to grab a few beers with him. We were always close, but being Mom's caretakers brought us even closer to one another. I definitely wanted to go have some beers with him and spend some quality time together. Why would I sit in the room when Mom was going to be sleeping? So, we tucked Mom into bed. I remember this clearly. Some would think this was a sweet little tuck in routine, putting her to rest after a long day, but this was far from the truth. Mom, as much as she has forgotten and tuned out from this horrible time of her life, still remembers that night we tucked her in. You see, because of her swollen ankles, we propped her feet up on pillows to raise them above her heart. We did this so the swelling would go down and return to normal size for the start of the next day. That night was a little different. Dad and I had a genius idea to get every pillow in the hotel room and stack them up. We then, as Mom puts it, "tortured her." Since we wanted to be sure she kept the pillows under her feet after we left the room, we took towels and tied her ankles to the pillows. Some would call this abuse, we thought of it as tough love. Away we went for some ice-cold Bud Lights :). Mom, sorry, but it worked and the next day you had your "sexy ankles" back. That was what we called them on her good days, when they stayed a normal size. Dad and I had a great time and still laugh to this day about it. During that trip to Vegas we felt normal again. Three months of the grueling battle were out of the way. A long journey was still ahead of us.

The holidays were approaching. Ever since I was little, I remember my mom loving Christmas and specifically the song, "We Need a Little Christmas." When she was just a young girl, her father passed away close to the holidays and her mother used to play that song to boost their spirits. I remember that year thinking, we really needed Christmas to come. We needed to have something else to look forward to. I rarely thought about my mother dying, but that holiday, I was actually feeling scared. Would it be our last Christmas as a family? Again, not something I usually thought about. In fact, I always tried to ignore the fact that people pass away from cancer and always told myself...nope, not my mom, but still every once in awhile I worried. Instead of a Christmas card that year, we made an "Elf" video, something so silly, but yet put a smile on all of our faces. It was an animated card in which we downloaded our pictures onto these elves bodies that then danced around and sang. We made one that had Mom, Dad, Matt and myself and passed it along to all our family and friends, thanking them for their prayers. We decided we needed a little laughter and did not want to deal with sending out traditional Christmas cards. However, we still wanted to wish everyone praying for our family a happy holiday!

December 10, 2008
Subject: Hahn update: December 10

Wonderful news!!! Prayers are being answered...keep 'em coming!!!!
Today they told us that Mom has a match and not only a match, a PERFECT match!!!
There is an amazing 42 yr old woman out there who matches Mom in

every aspect. The transplant will be scheduled for sometime in January, approximately 4 weeks from now!!!

Mom is currently on day 2 of her fifth cycle of chemo. We will be in the hospital until Saturday night. We will go home, her counts will drop to zero and recover, same old routine.

We will then enjoy Christmas and have something special to celebrate!
Love to all!!! CAN YOU BELIEVE PERFECT MATCH?!?!?!?! Oh, the power of prayer!!!

Ash

Woohoo! It was just in time for the holidays. See...there is a Santa! Knowing Mom had found a perfect match was a relief. The next round of chemo would be a little bit easier knowing we had an answer. Before we knew it, we would be scheduled for the transplant. Not only did I have a "Santa" moment with my mom finding a match, but also a friend of my dad's sent me a check for the holidays. The check was enough to cover the next six months of my bills. Although I was on family medical leave, I still had to pay for my own health insurance, make car payments, as well as pay my cell phone and auto insurance bills. That year "Santa" was overly generous.
*On a side note....if you ever find yourself going through a situation similar to ours, please remember that the time frame the doctors give you is always a "guess." Things tend to take a little longer on the medical side than what they plan. You will see what I mean in the chapters ahead.

December 18, 2008
Subject: Hahn Update December 18th

Mark your calendars. We officially have a date! Mom will be admitted on January 29th or 30th for a week of new chemo followed by a February 6th transplant. Until then, love to all and Happy Holidays!!!

-Ash

Most people during the holiday season are stressing over whose house to visit and what to buy for the holidays. The Hahn family on the other hand, was planning for the biggest day of my mom's life (aside from her wedding and the days that Matt and I were born of course). With knowing there was an end in sight, our Christmas 2008 was very nice. We already had a lot to celebrate. We were looking forward to the transplant and Mom getting better. Of course, at the same time we were anxious and unsure of what lay ahead.

If you are in this situation, I must warn you that once you have a transplant date, the patient is basically given a full-time job of attending appointment after appointment. In order to undergo a transplant, one must be examined from head to toe. You see every doctor imaginable and are administered a wide array of examinations and tests. We saw cardiologists, primary care physicians, dentists, eye doctors, the works.

CHAPTER 10: JANUARY 2009- PREPPING FOR OUR BIG DAY

"Nobody can go back and start a new beginning, but anyone can start today and make a new ending." –Maria Robinson

January 15, 2009
Subject: Hahn Update Jan 15

Hey everyone....I'm sure you missed me!!!

Just a little update. After two weeks of testing Mom from head to toe, from the dentist, to her lungs, her heart to her bone marrow, she is "Perfect, extraordinary and wonderful." We even had one doc tell us she is as "healthy as a horse." Hmmmmmm........funny how someone can be doing so great and yet working on their second cancer.... boy, they can make you laugh.

Anyway, in all seriousness....Mom is doing REALLY well. She is scheduled to be admitted on January 29th and we can expect to be in the hospital for 30 days and then released as daily outpatients. It will be a long journey. We have to work up to day 100...the first good sign that her body accepted someone else's immune system. Until then, Mom and I are headed to Tampa for a 4-night trip in which she can soak up the sun and get pumped for her new 42 year old marrow!!!!

Love to all
Ash

What a whirlwind. In a two-week period, we went to what felt like a million doctors' appointments. Mom and I deserved a break! Remember, in between chemo rounds, Mom always hit a point when she was feeling absolutely "normal." Thank goodness we had that time before the actual transplant. We needed to unwind and not think about anything. Mom had not had a treatment since before the holidays and was feeling good. Time to party!

A dear friend helped us go on a trip and arranged an amazing place to stay, which was a lot of fun! Mom, her friend Cher, my Aunt Cathy and I met up at a casino in Tampa, Florida, where we played cards, slots and enjoyed a day at the spa. We laughed a lot, had some drinks and just loved the feeling of freedom. I remember one day, we all sat down at a three card poker table. We spontaneously started the "wave" around the table. One after another, we threw our arms into the air, leaned back and yelled, "wooooo." So silly, yet so fun. Some people may have thought we were crazy, but we were just having a good time. Smiling, laughing, and sharing time with friends is a simple joy that is often taken for granted.

Mom was appreciative of each and every minute of her time away from the hospital. Even though the transplant was around the corner, Tampa made us forget about it. We were so pre-occupied with the sun and fun that we didn't think about it. Even at night, we laid in bed like little schoolgirls gossiping and laughing. One night we laughed so hard that we were all in tears. Cher continued day after day, telling us she never sleeps at night. Well one night, she was snoring so loudly within five minutes of her head hitting the pillow, that my mom, aunt and I thought we would pee our pants. We were laughing so hard and joking with one another that she was full of it. The next morning we told her our story. She seemed well rested. As we left Tampa to head home, Mom and I said to one another, "Can't we stay?" As anxious as we were to get on with the transplant, we loved our time away in Florida!

January 29, 2009
Subject: Hahn Update Jan. 29

Hey everyone! Just wanted to let you know that we have checked back into Ruby Hospital Bone Marrow Unit aka Mom's spa/resort for a month!!! Mom successfully had a new line placed into her chest this morning. It is called a triple hickman lumen...they put her under and the surgery went very well. She is now settled into her room with some ice on her chest and is taking a little snooze.

For the rest of the day today, they will be pumping her with some premeds for the chemo. Specifically, one that prevents seizures. She will take these pills throughout the day today.

Tomorrow, Friday the 30th, Saturday the 31st and Sunday Feb 1, she will receive chemo treatments.

Monday, February 2nd will be a very tough day in which she receives a chemo drug that comes from a rabbit...yes, a rabbit...she may be hopping around the hospital, twitching her nose, begging for carrots. Seriously though, this will probably be her worst day up here. They said she would feel horrible, flu like symptoms and think she cannot make it. She is well aware of this and is telling the docs, "Fine...but all you get is one day of me feeling sick!"

Tuesday, Feb 3rd she will feel 50% better and Wed. even better. (still getting rabbit juice those two days, but with fewer side effects)

Thursday, Feb 5th will be a day of rest, without any chemo! AND Friday, Feb 6th is the big day....with the transplant.

After that, we can expect to be in the hospital for 3-4 more weeks.

Please continue to keep her in your prayers!!!!

You may send cards to the house and/or emails to my account. If you are in town, please stop by. She would LOVE visitors any day other than Mon. the 2nd.

Love to all.... BIG HUGS!!!
Ash

January 29th was the day I officially freaked out! The plan was in place. There was no turning back. Everything we had done to prepare Mom for the transplant paled in comparison to the next few days in the hospital, let alone the 100 that followed. I remember thinking here goes nothing. I was dreading the sound of Monday, February 2nd. "Rabbit Juice," sounded potent. Something I would never wish upon my worst enemy.

CHAPTER 11: FEBRUARY 2009- TRANSPLANT MONTH

Lance Armstrong once said, "Birthdays don't really matter much anymore...for me, I sort of have a new birthday."

February was the month Mom was going to have a new birthday to celebrate.

February 3, 2009
Subject: Hahn Update Feb 3

Hey all!

Don't let those cute bunnies fool you!!! In fact...I wouldn't mind it if I never saw a rabbit again!!!!

As you know, we checked in the hospital last Thursday. The weekend chemo went really well without any side effects. HOWEVER......
Yesterday was her first day of the lovely "rabbit juice" medicine. Its job is to knock out Mom's entire immune system so that she can accept someone else's to replace hers. Well....last night definitely proved that the med was working. Mom vomited all night and around 4 a.m. spiked a

temperature that was close to 103 degrees. Do not be alarmed though...this is all very common. We were just hoping she wouldn't feel quite so bad. They packed her in ice to bring her fever down and she was all right by 8 a.m. today. When she isn't getting sick, she is sleeping soundly from all of the other drugs they have given her. When she gets up to use the bathroom, she staggers like a drunken sailor. One nurse said that she must be "a cheap date!" I honestly do not know if she knows what is going on. She definitely feels very sick at times, but it is so brief and by the time everything is cleaned up she is sleeping again. We want to keep it that way throughout the next two days.

Mom will receive more of this NASTY medicine today and tomorrow. They are going to continue to pump her with anti-nausea medicine. They told us we can expect the same side effects today, but hopefully tomorrow will be much better.

Thursday, she will not have any medicine or chemo. They are calling it her day of rest. Matt will be coming into town on Thursday to be with us Friday for the transplant and stay the weekend. I will probably send an email out tomorrow sometime. Please continue to pray. She is doing very well even though she doesn't think so. I feel so bad for her, yet she is being such a trooper!!!

Love to all,
Ash

Out of EVERYTHING Mom endured throughout her treatment, I can assure you that February 2nd was the worst! The first night Mom was administered the "Rabbit Juice," I stayed with her all night, and thank God I did. She was completely unaware of what was happening to her, she vomited uncontrollably, her whole body shook from a high fever and she was unable to communicate coherently. She was only able to stay awake just long enough to get sick, before she would pass out again. To see your mother packed in ice and so sick is a horrible feeling. You wish you were the one who could take her pain away and not let her suffer. She did not want to keep fighting that night. She told me, "I've had enough." I just kept holding her hand and telling her it would be over soon. Although for that 24 hour-plus period, I never thought it would end. The next morning, I kept thinking, does she have to take more of this potent drug? How could they? It seemed like mere torture. I thanked God that day one was finally over! The doctors were right; day two was much better.

February 4, 2009
Subject: Quick Hahn Update Feb 4

GOOOOOODDDD Morning!!!

Mom took that rabbit juice like a champ yesterday! No fever, no vomiting and she slept through the night.

She woke up and showered, was able to walk one lap of the hall, ate a piece of toast and is back in bed for the day. Snoozing already!!! You probably will not hear from me until after the transplant. Please keep her in your prayers. One more day of rabbit juice today (fingers crossed it goes as well as yesterday), one day of rest tomorrow and transplant Friday night. Love to all!
Ash

I told you Mom was a trooper. Knocked on her ass one day and back up on her feet the next. I am so thankful that she did not clearly remember the details of the first night of the "juice." Day two she was back up and at 'em. Another plug here....Remember, no matter how much you or the patient do not want to get up and walk, do it! My mother walked every chance she got. Even if she didn't feel well, my dad and I pushed her to walk at least one lap around the unit. I swear this was the key to getting out of the hospital as fast as we did. Patients cannot lie there no matter how bad they feel. As sick as Mom was the night before, she got up and moved the next day.
It was two days until the BIG DAY. Wow! We had made it. Now what would lie ahead? We kept wondering...what would it be like? They said it would be just a drip. Would it? How long would it take? Where was the marrow coming from? Would Mom accept it? There were so many unanswered questions, but at the same time, there was so much to look forward to.

February 6, 2009
Subject: Hahn Update-Transplant Day

Hey Everyone!

The big day has finally arrived. We are told the transplant will be around 10 p.m. tonight. Therefore, you will not hear from me until tomorrow. I just didn't want everyone wondering/worrying all day. The transplant itself is very easy. It comes in a bag, is hung on the ceiling and slowly drips into her line through her chest. There is no pain involved; in fact, they say people often sleep right through them. Say a little prayer tonight!!!

Love to all,
Ash

February 6th was one of the longest days of my life. We waited around all day long. I wanted to do something to celebrate, so I went to Michaels to pick up some cheap toasting flutes. I then went to the local grocery store to grab some sparkling cider (I did not think using an alcoholic beverage like champagne would be a good idea minutes before the much anticipated transplant). We planned to say a toast right before the transplant. All day long, Mom, Dad, Matt and I sat and watched the clock tick away.

I kept opening and shutting the door to look down the long white hallway. It was close to the time when the doctors told us to expect the cells. I don't know what I was expecting, but I kept thinking they would come down the hall in a dramatic fashion (like you see in the movies). Well, for all of those who have never seen a bone marrow transplant, it comes in a bag just like blood or platelets would and simply hangs on a pole and slowly drips. The whole bone marrow process takes only about an hour and the patient doesn't feel a thing. There is a nurse in with you the whole time. We sat as a family and prayed that this would be the cure. This would be a miracle. Mom would begin a new life!

February 7, 2009
Subject: Hahn Update: Post Transplant

Good Morning!!!

I know everyone is anxious to hear about last night. Mom's transplant went well. They called around 8 pm to tell us the cells had arrived and the labs had to work with them for a while. Around 10:30, Matt, Dad, and I pulled out little champagne glasses and sparkling cider and did a toast to a new year, a new birthday, and a continued fight until we get through it all! There were both smiles and tears.

Around 11:00, the cells were hung and began to drip slowly into Mom. By 12:00, it was over and she was able to get a good night's rest.

A new journey has begun. This first part will be very hard on her. Mom's white blood cell count is at zero right now. She does not have a lot of energy. For the next two to three weeks, we will wait for her count to recover and the new cells to multiply and spread throughout her marrow. It is important she walks everyday to jump-start the cells and get them moving in the right direction. There will be days, in the next two weeks, where she is very sick with fevers, vomiting, diarrhea and mouth sores. They will continue to give her meds to help prevent and/or lessen the side effects.

Once we are able to go home, I will continue to take her to the hospital everyday to be checked out and for some replacements such as blood transfusions, etc. Once she is no longer dependent on the replacements, we will start to go twice a week, then once a week and so forth until she no longer has to be seen by the docs.

Surprisingly though, our doc told Mom that she may be able to go to the NCAA tournament this year with a mask on. No pressure Dad and Matt!!!!! :)

Thank you for the continued prayers during our long journey. I probably will not send another update for a few days now. Take care....cards and emails are still welcomed and greatly appreciated. If you would like to come visit us in room 920, please call my cell ahead (Phone number listed here). If you are sick or have been around anyone who is sick, please wait awhile before stopping by. Thanks again!!! Mom has had a few visitors already, including some of Dad's basketball players, and it sure brightens her day!

Love to all and BIG HUGS!!!
Ash

February 13, 2009
Subject: Hahn Update Feb. 13

Shoulda known today, when I woke up and realized it was Friday the 13th, that we were in for a haywire day. The expected side effects have arrived. Mom is feeling pretty crummy today. She has mouth sores that lead all the way down her throat and probably through her colon. She describes it as the worst strep throat ever! It is hard for her to swallow. In fact, she is no longer able to take her medicine by mouth and all of her pills have to be pumped through an IV or one of her three lines. Also, she is dealing with nausea. She cannot take a sip of water without throwing up. They have given her a morphine pump to use as needed and several drugs to stop the "sick" feeling. They have appeared to work. She is sleeping every chance she gets, although they are slim and few b/c there is always someone in here hanging a new drug or checking her temp, etc. The side effects will slowly go away as her count recovers. Right now, it is at zero and can be there for a few days, but the good news is, there is no where to go but up from here! Take care. Love to all.

Ash

Friday the 13th is such a superstitious day. Never before had I cared about whether or not the 13th of a month fell on a Friday. That Friday the 13th was terrible for me. As I read through my emails again, I could see that although I was feeling down that day, as I watched my mother suffer from the transplant, I kept a somewhat positive attitude. I ended the email with "there is no where to go but up from here!" When going through the grueling process of fighting any cancer, there are times when you are so exhausted, burnt out, and flat out sick. That was one of those days. I remember thinking how many drugs can they keep pumping into my mom? How is her body handling all of this?

Mouth sores, a severe sore throat and nausea were my mother's main side effects on that Friday the 13th. I knew we had to expect side effects, but I truly believed that the side effects were my mom's way of her body saying that it had, had enough. Her body was trying to tell her to "Cut the shit." :)

I believe it was during this long stay in the hospital that I had set up our chain link system. As we had done in the past with the post its, we were going to count down the days until we got the heck out of the hospital. I sat one morning, probably a week prior to transplant, cutting strips of yellow and blue papers. I strung them together in a chain link pattern, which hung from the ceiling and dangled all the way down to the floor. The colors we used were yellow and blue for West Virginia. Go Eers! Every night before Dad or I left, we would pull off a link and do a little silly dance for Mom. We would dance that piece of paper all the way to the closest trashcan; happily knowing one more day was behind us. The doctors and nurses all knew our rule; Mom was to get out of the hospital before all of the links were gone. Remember, she is an overachiever. She was determined not to stay the entire time they had predicted. Somehow, someway, she always found a way to get home early.

February 21, 2009
Subject: Hahn Update-Feb 21.

Greetings from (our address went here)....yes you read that correctly....we are HOME!!!!!!!!!!!!!!

Mom checked out of the hospital around 1:00 today. We are home, ate some lunch, and are watching Matt's game on TV right now. She is so happy to be here :)

So here's the deal...Mom's counts have gone up pretty quickly. She is still complaining of a very sore throat. We will be taking about 20 pills a day, but the thought of good night's sleep keeps us going!!! I will take Mom into the hospital as an outpatient for the next 100 days. It will begin as a daily trip and will soon become less frequent.

They will be watching her very closely now for GVHD (Graft vs. host disease). The signs can range from a skin rash to something more severe. GVHD occurs if her body begins to reject the transplant. It is a very scary thing, HOWEVER, a little bit of it is okay and can be controlled. Keep praying for a fast recovery and acceptance of the marrow.

Uncle Tim (my mom's brother) will be coming today until next Saturday. It will be nice to have him around to help for a full week.

We cannot begin to thank you for everything so far from prayers, to cards, to all of the goodies. I will continue to keep you posted on our next part of the journey. We are almost done!!!!! 100 days out without any problems will be our goal....she is already 14 days :) Only 86 to go!!! WE CAN DO IT!!!

Love to all,
Ash

I remember thinking, "Oh my gosh, could I take care of my mom for the next 100 days? What was going to happen?" Dad and I had read up on all of the discharge information and had both passed a written test to be Mom's caretakers. We had all the supplies we needed at home, and thanks to Aunt Barbara, we had an amazing weekly pill container labeled with every day of the week. Under each day were sub categories, a.m., noon, evening and p.m. This was a lifesaver. In addition to sorting the pills out in those containers, I also took each bottle the pills came in (remember there were 20 different pills she took a day) and labeled them with a permanent marker. I labeled the times that each specific pill was to be taken. All of the bottles stood upright in a cute little Vera Bradley bag that we purchased strictly for Mom's medicine. This was my "OCD" way of controlling the pills. It really worked! I would fill the pill box a week at a time. I opened all of the compartments, grabbed one pill bottle at a time, read the label that I had written on the top and dispensed the pills accordingly. After all of my mom's hard work in the hospital, I was not going to be the one to screw up her medicine and land her back in there. One missed pill and she could be very sick. Not on my watch!

It was so good to be home. However, it was frustrating knowing we would be an outpatient every single day for another 100 days. I knew it was what we had to do though. To help us get going, Mom and I sang silly songs every morning, for example, "whoa-oh-oh-oh, I don't want to go!" We knew we had to go though, so we just kept trekking on.

CHAPTER 12: MARCH 2009- MARCH MADNESS?

Tommy Lasorda shared, "The difference between the impossible and the possible lies in a man's determination."

March 2, 2009
Subject: Hahn Update-March 2nd

Hey everyone!

It has been awhile since I have sent an email. We have REALLY been enjoying our time at home. It makes such a big difference sleeping in our own beds and having our own showers. :)

The last 10 days could be compared to a roller coaster ride. Let me explain...

We came home and for the first several days, we were on the climb up the hill to feeling better. Mom felt terrible. She battled nausea, with both vomiting and diarrhea. She could not eat, had trouble drinking b/c she would throw it up, struggled to take pills, and started to get a rash all over her body.

Then one day, during one of our daily trips in, they decided that Mom had some Graft Vs Host Disease, which caused all of the problems above. GVHD is when her old cells start to fight the new cells and do not want them in her body. As their first line of defense, they started her on a steroid and the very next day she became a new lady. We were on our way down the hill to smooth sailing.

Mom started to eat little meals. She took her pills like a champ and was able to drink a lot of fluids. Her throat was even healed from the sores and she was no longer in pain.

For the last 4 days or so, things have been going great. Then yesterday, we started that climb again. I have never been so scared in my entire life. Mom had taken a shower and was sitting on the side of the tub putting her pjs on. She told me she wanted to get in bed. Before she even finished getting dressed, her eyes rolled in the back of her head and she passed out. All I could see was the white of her eyes. I was screaming at her to wake up and holding her body up since it went limp. What seemed like forever, probably lasted 15 seconds, she looked back at me and said, "Can we please go to bed?" She had no idea this had happened. Before I could explain, she went back out. Her eyes in the same position, all of her body weight on me. I got her lying down and continued to try to have her come to. I ran to the phone and called 911, as well as a neighbor. The second one again, seemed like forever, but probably lasted 30 seconds this time. When she woke up, she asked why she was laying on the floor and why the neighbor was there. We explained it and she did not recall any of it. The EMTS came and evaluated her. They immediately said they did NOT think she seizured, but blacked out due to a drastic drop in her blood pressure (possibly from the heat of the shower and the bathroom being too hot.)

To their surprise, as always, Mom over-achieved. She stood herself up and walked down our stairs. She told them she really felt good and did not want to go back in. She had to though, so they then put her on a stretcher and I followed the ambulance. We did not go to the ER b/c of all of the germs they took us up to our Bone Marrow Unit. Mom was admitted and will remain in the hospital either until today or tomorrow. They think it was all probably caused by some sort of infection and have run several tests such as blood cultures, heart test, chest x-ray, etc. It may be from that same line that gave us problems once before. They have started her on fluids in case it was dehydration and two new antibiotics to start to fight the infection, wherever the source may be.

I should have more info soon. Mom is feeling great and really doesn't want to be in there right now. Like I said, she really does not remember it, so she was not very affected by it. Me, on the other hand...well, I keep picturing it over and over again. I will NOT be home alone with Mom again for a very long time. She really scared me this time.

Love to all,
Ash

PS- My uncle was a huge help! I was even able to get out for a massage one day and a haircut another. I hit the gym several times and loved having someone else around at all times. Let me know if you want to volunteer some time here. :)

Hugs!!!

I know in a previous chapter I said the "Rabbit Juice" was the worst night ever, however, that 911-phone call, lies neck and neck with that. I was home alone with my mom when the blackouts happened and I had never been so scared. I felt that I handled the situation well, but did not want anything like that to ever happen again. I was afraid to be home alone with her for a while afterward. Still to this day, 2 years out, I sometimes have nightmares and relive that moment. I cannot thank my neighbor Eddie enough for coming over and just being with me until the ambulance arrived. I remember my mom looking at Eddie and looking at me like, "What the heck are we all doing here laying on the bathroom floor?" Since my mom only had a towel to cover her, Eddie left the room for a moment so I could get her into her "jammies" before the paramedics arrived. My mom is a beautiful woman and once again, did not like to be seen if she wasn't looking her best.

I was so relieved when I saw the ambulance pull up because I knew if she passed out again there would be professionals there to care for her. She made us all laugh as she walked herself down the stairs to the stretcher. On the way to the hospital, they made me follow behind the ambulance. She called me from her cell phone and told me she better not miss Dad's game. She was a little perturbed I was taking her in. My mom did not know how scared I was. She did not even remember anything that happened. I know she was questioning why she was being taken to the hospital. I cannot blame her for wanting to stay home after all the time she had spent in the hospital, but I wanted her to have a full check up.

March 6, 2009
Subject: Quick Hahn Update

I forgot to let everyone know we are out of the hospital. They only kept us Sunday until Tuesday. All of the tests have come back negative; therefore, they are blaming the black out on dehydration and LOW blood pressure.

Yesterday morning, Mom had three more black out spells. Thank goodness, Dad was home!!! We got her into our outpatient area where they pumped her with fluids...again dehydrated.

Today, Thursday, she has NOT had any episodes and is doing well. She feels like she is floating b/c I am practically pouring water down her throat.

Her best friend from MD, Cher, has been here for a few days. Big Help. Dad's family is coming for the weekend and one of my aunts will be here the following week. It makes all the difference in the world!
Love to all,
Ash

I was usually so quick to send an update every time we got out of the hospital, but at that time it took a few days because the black outs really freaked me out. There was no rhyme or reason when she would "go down" on us. I laugh now because when I use this phrase, my friends say, "it just doesn't sound right, saying your mom goes down on you." Typical guy friends, so immature, but so funny. Anyway, out of nowhere, Mom would get this blank look in her eyes and the next thing you know she was passing out. The only thing we could do was catch her to lessen the fall, lay her on her back, raise her feet above her heart, and turn her head to the side so that she didn't swallow her tongue. Yes, that's right; when someone passes out they can choke on their own tongue from it rolling back into their throat.

By no means would Dad and I have known all of this without our neighbor Cathy down the street. Cathy was a nurse. She was amazing during the whole recovery process. Every time Mom passed out, I would freak out and call Cathy. She would run down the street with her blood pressure cuff in hand, and check on Mom. This unfortunately became a little too routine for us. No matter what time of day, Cathy would always show up in minutes. She was amazing. It also helped that her husband was previously the pharmacist for the bone marrow unit. He too gave us a lot of guidance during Mom's recovery. I felt so much better with my dad around and/or the neighbors when one of the "episodes," as I started to call them, occurred.

March 15, 2009
Subject: Hahn Update-March 15th

Hey everyone! Some good news first, followed by a little bad and then some more good.

Good News:
We have not had a blackout episode since last Tuesday :) PHEW!!! She

has started to eat more and more each day with her taste buds slowly returning and very little nausea (other than when she takes her 20 pills a day) AND

To our surprise, yesterday, Saturday, they gave her a "day off." We did not have to report to the hospital for our outpatient visit. It was so nice to sleep in and Mom stayed in jammies all day :)

Bad News:
Mom is battling discomfort with her skin. Under her armpits, chest, and hands have begun to peel away the old layers of skin. It is raw and hurts her. We alternate between putting a special powder and cream on throughout the day. They assure us this also happens and will hopefully last only a week. They compare it to the worst sunburn ever...where is turns bright red and burns, peels off and then recovers. Mom continues to need to be pumped with fluids daily, which is very common.

Good News:
We had a nice visit with my Aunt Cathy. In fact, she did such a great job we have invited her back. I am covered with family and friends up until March 30th. It is a relief for me to know there is always someone around in case anything happens, especially with Dad traveling so much right now.

Tonight is Selection Sunday and the NCAA bracket will be announced. Dad's team is meeting to watch the show and we are going to take Mom along to enjoy the company of the players and share their excitement! She is looking forward to her little outing.

Hope all is well with everyone. Love to all.
Ash

Rereading the above email, I have to laugh at myself when I chose to use the following format for my updates: good news, bad news, good news. This is a strategy teachers use during parent teacher conferences when talking about a student. They begin their meeting with the parents discussing something positive, hit them with any areas of concern, and finish up on a positive note. My emails followed this format and it still makes me laugh :).

So, yay to no blackouts! However, the new skin issue was horrific. Mom would lose all of her old skin and re-grow new skin. I remember it got so bad. My poor mother had to have been in a ton of pain. Layers of skin would come off and all that was left was raw, moist and bloody surfaces. All we could do was simply put ointment and/or powder on it and try to comfort her. Her skin was shedding everywhere. Little brown flakes of her skin covered her bed, the chair she sat in, her clothes and virtually everything she touched. It hurt her to shower, it hurt her to sit, and sleeping was even a challenge. Every single morning Dad would stand by Mom's side in the bathroom while she brushed her teeth and got dressed. Meanwhile, I would secretly strip the bed, run downstairs, stain stick all of the bloodstained sheets, and pray they would come out white again. We actually used some hospital sheets during that time so we didn't ruin Mom and Dad's nice ones.

When we had bad days, we just prayed that some good news would follow. Somehow just one little good report seemed to wipe away the bad days. A good report meant encouragement and a lift in spirits. Although Mom rarely let you see her get down, we just knew she felt relieved and hopeful any time good news came. Two days after that email about the skin, we got just that, positive news! Some say it could have been the luck of the Irish (Mom is Irish), but that St. Patty's Day a toast was in order!

March 17, 2009
Subject: AWESOME NEWS

Mom took a test a week ago and we got the results yesterday. She is 100% donor. Her old immune system has been replaced with the donor's!!! Great news!!!!

She has had a smile on her face all day. The doctors gave us today and Friday off to sleep in and relax!!! Prayers are working.

Love to all!!!
Big Cheers! Toast on St Patty's to Mom!
Ash

Mom was doing it! Her body had accepted her donor's marrow and although she was going through terrible side effects, the transplant had done its job. I loved the days that we received good news because everyone shared the pleasure of hearing something positive. The positive news trickled down from her to me, to my dad, to my fiancé, to all of the people reading the emails and so on. The good news always came with wonderful email responses that I always shared with Mom. You could see how proud of herself she was. She should have been too. It takes a strong, courageous person not to give up when the going gets tough. We were getting closer and closer to my wedding.

March 26, 2009
Subject: Hahn Update-March 26

Hey everyone!

Mom is 48 days out of transplant. We are almost halfway done with the road to recovery.

Unfortunately, a lot has happened in the 10 days since my last email. We need your help again with the power of prayer.

Mom has had a tough stretch. Her skin is so raw. It is hard to describe, other than comparing it to you falling down and scraping your knee on cement. It is so painful for her and often bleeds. The main spots are her armpits, under her boobs and her bottom. She is very uncomfortable. We have tried 5 different strategies and just today seem to be seeing slight improvement. We are waiting for her new skin to grow. She has to sit and sleep on an egg crate foam mattress pad and everything she wears soaks through with either the ointment/blood or a combo. It takes a lot for her to get comfortable. The latest they tried was a new pain medicine; well four doses later and two episodes of vomiting after taking it, we are off that drug! (This is from that darn rabbit juice pre-transplant). They are hoping it will be cleared in a few days.

In addition to the skin, she continues to need fluids about every other day. Since she is weak and dehydrated, we must walk with her wherever she goes (bathroom, steps, car, hallway, etc). She has not fully blacked out in about 10 days, but has had two close calls in which we got her laying down and feet up just in time to prevent it.

Lastly, they are testing for a virus, which is very common with transplant patients. If mom has it, they will need to see us everyday two times a day. Please pray for good results...we are still waiting this outcome.

Some good news....Dad is home more now. He has been a HUGE help and it is so nice to have his support and comfort knowing he is here at all times. We have had some super help over the last few weeks. Mom's friend Joni, my dad's brother Jim and my dad's sister Cathy. My friend Lisa just came in today for the weekend.

Matt will be coming to town Monday for over a week. Between him and Dad, I am going to try to brave it and head to MD. I need a break and I think Mom is probably sick of me.

Love to all...sorry we don't have better news. Miss everyone...let me know if you wanna come help out.

Ash

Halfway to the 100 day mark. Pretty darn good! Only halfway and I had already needed a break. I remember literally having to "let go" for the few trips when I went back to Maryland. I knew I had to do it, to see Brian and my friends, as well as get a break from being a caregiver, but it was so scary to "let go." I guess even though I don't have children, this must be how a parent feels when they leave their baby with someone else for the first time. Between Matt and Dad, I knew Mom would be fine, but you better believe before I left every pill was organized and labeled. I also left a long list of directions for the boys to follow. I wish I had a camera in the house when I was away. Poor Matt, I don't think a son ever thinks he will have to rub his mom's skin with ointment, but he did it like a champ and really stepped up to the plate and helped.

Anyone who cannot be around a loved one during a difficult time knows how hard it is and how guilty you feel that you are away. Matt often felt so helpless knowing he was all the way in Vermont and receiving the same email updates others were. He checked in at least three times a day and was constantly calling Dad and I for reports, as well as asking to talk to Mom. He is a "momma's boy." Somehow, regardless of whether Mom was having a good or bad day, just hearing from him made her smile. It was nice that he could actually be around for a while.

Every year we look forward to the start of basketball season, but we also look forward to it ending. It is nice to have the guys around more. Basketball coaches are constantly on the go, yet there is the tiniest bit of down period after the season before camps and recruiting begins. It was so nice to spend time as a family before I left for Maryland. I stayed a few days so Matt and I would overlap and he could learn our routine.

March 31st was a special day. We received a letter from our donor. Depending on the registry, you cannot have phone or email contact with your donor for at least a year. In Mom's case, it was two years. The only thing they could do in the meantime was write hand-written letters back and forth. Even still, they really hid the donor's identity. All of the letters had to go through the bone marrow office and they examined what was written before exchanging them. For example, the first letter was in the donor's handwriting and in an envelope, however, the envelope was completely blacked out where the postage was as well as any other personal information. Completely blocked. I of course, would still hold each letter up to the sunlight to try to see through the permanent marker. It didn't work out in my favor though. So when our first letter had arrived, I immediately sent an email to all of our family and friends. I typed word for word what the donor had written.

March 31, 2009
Subject: Letter from donor!

Hey all...wanted to share something special with you.

When mom got her transplant, she was able to write the donor a thank you letter. Today, Monday, March 30th, we heard back from our donor. She seems to be a very lovely lady. We cannot wait to meet her. We cannot exchange any specific info until one year out. 313 more days and mom and I will be hopping a plane to who knows where....you can see from the letter, our donor appears to be foreign. Any guesses? (by the way, map in the letter refers to the card mom wrote her, and she says his a lot for her).

I will tell you mom had her biggest meal the other night, 3 helpings of shrimp lo mein!!! We have fought her to even eat one helping, let alone three!! I think she is a Chinese lady.

As for an update: skin is SLOWLY improving, docs think one more week. We have to begin to treat a virus that is common post transplant. She will need a special med via IV two times a day. We are looking into getting at home care for one of the doses.

I am off to MD. Matt and Dad are here until Friday on duty!

Love to all,
Ash

Donor's letter can be found below:

Hello ???

At first many thanks for your card! I was frightened as so soon a letter came from the Center. As I have seen the map, I started to tremble and after the first reading my feeling were overwhelmed because the whole time when in November 2008 first time I was called for the blood-disease, I thought "yes I would like to help, it can be used for someone like me: a mother. This person/patient hopes to life and to see his children to grow up."

In the whole research and preparations, I always have thought, yes I do it and believe it.

My son (9 years) said once: "Mummy, why are you doing this actually, can not make someone else this, I have to fear for you?"

I tried to explain him that it is for someone, who perhaps has children. I want to help this person, and also to help to see his children grow up.

Many friends said: "That's great it would greatly be which I would make there for a strange human." But it was correct for me and I had it never felt in such a way.

And the confirmation came with your map. Yes, it was correctly hurts to bear. How are you? I would also like to know gladly much about you.

I think I may write (the rules keep?), I'm 42 years and have 3 lovely, great kids (2 girls 16 and 13 years arduously and a son 9 years), I'm divorced, but had a very wonderful, loving partner and it supported me in everything and still does.

You write me you consider me your guardian angel, but I think we both have perhaps the same guardian angel on our watch?! I think a lot of you, pray for you and wish myself and you that it concerns you well to see growing up your daughter/children. I hope you write me again and in my letter are not so many errors, my English isn't good.

With lovely greetings

Yours ??? :)

That first exchange was very special. It brought happy tears to all. What an amazing woman, with children of her own, reaching out to help a total stranger. Mom was excited to be a "young 42-year-old woman." The donor was definitely a guardian angel and we couldn't wait to learn more about her. I remember always hoping the cancer center would have another letter for us, but they did not come often. It is much easier to stay in touch with our donor today, since we can now use email. Towards the end of the book, I will share the most up to date exchanges.

CHAPTER 13: APRIL 2009- AMAZING FRIENDS AND FAMILY

A famous poet, Eustache Deschamps, shared that, "Friends are relatives you make for yourself."

April 7, 2009
Subject: Hahn Update-April 7

Hey Everyone!!!

Just wanted to let you all know our latest.

Matt was here for a week and I was able to get home to MD for 3 days. He did a tremendous job once he realized you don't wash fruit with soap and water haha. :) He was amazing with mom. Dad and Matt were hanging IVs, treating her skin, doing laundry, cooking meals and loading/unloading the dishwasher. They were a great team!!!

Mom is still battling the skin issue. Her armpits have cleared completely and her boobs and bottom are continuing to heal. Slow process, but the areas are getting smaller and smaller. She is still bleeding a lot and it is painful.

We continue to treat the virus I mentioned before. An at home care nurse came to the house and taught Dad and Matt how to give Mom the IV. Since I have been back, I learned too! We administer it two times a day on our days off and only at night the days we go to the hospital. Her virus count was at 42,000 and with 6 days of the drug has dropped to 6,000. We should continue this drug for 2 more weeks.

Unfortunately, with this drug, the black out episodes have returned. They think it's a combo of all of the drugs. She has had two fainting incidents when Matt was here. Both occurred at the hospital. They do not seem worried about it, but it freaks us out!!! Hopefully, as they wean her off some of her other drugs, they will disappear.

Mom's spirits are a little down. She is still being a fighter and not complaining, but sadder at night asking when this will all be over. We all feel that way right now....just want it to be over and mom back to normal. Keep praying!!!

Love to all,
Ash

Funny story to go with the email above: Although not funny at the time, it is now. Matt shared the story with me of when Mom passed out on him. I guess he had taken her into the hospital for the outpatient services and she needed to use the restroom. Well, when they got into the stall, she blacked out. This is what made me laugh. My brother, a six-foot tall man, said he, "yelled like a bitch." Supposedly, he started screaming like a girl as he called for the nurses. I wish I could have seen him. I know first hand how scary it was, so I do not blame him one bit. At least his encounter with Mom's blackouts happened at the hospital with doctors and nurses around. I can still picture him screaming now. :)

April 14, 2009
Subject: Hahn Update April 14

Hey everyone!

Just a bit of info for you:

Mom continues to battle the raw skin, but it has improved a lot. The doctors say between two and three more weeks before it is completely healed. We continue to put special cream and pads on it two times a day.

We continue to treat the CMV virus with two IV drips a day. I administer them at the house on our days off. We need the numbers to keep dropping so we can stop this nasty drug.

We are still going into the hospital 4 days a week and are LOVING our 3 days off.

Mom's last black out episode was Monday, April 6th. Last Thursday we met with the doctor and we described the episodes we have had (a total of ten). I told him how Mom is walking, stops, stares off and goes out. When she comes to, she doesn't even know anything happened. He informed me that I had described to him an "absence seizure." These can occur from two of the million of drugs Mom is currently on. We began treating them with a new drug she takes twice a day. We have not had any problems since we started the drug other then a moment of complete weakness when she got to the top of the steps Easter Sunday and her legs buckled. She swears she was not fully out, but I think she may have been for a few seconds. We will continue to pray this new drug works.

LASTLY:

I think Mom may need a little pick-me up, therefore, we are going to open our house to visitors in the evening from 7-7:30. There will be some rules.
-Please make sure you are free of germs and haven't been around anyone who is sick.
-No kids allowed
-Visits must be brief
-Please do not bring anything with you!!!!

Thanks guys! I think hearing a new voice and seeing some faces other than Dad's and mine will bring some new energy to the house.

Love to all,
Ash

Day in and day out, seeing the same people and having nothing new to talk about got old. It was important to allow people to visit even if we were scared they would bring germs with them. New voices and stories really made a difference. Several neighbor ladies, my mom's friends Renee and Kay, and others stopped by after my email. Most people who came shared that they had wanted to come by earlier, but were scared to bother us. I am glad they came because even though they were short visits, they meant a lot to all of us.

Another person who really touched our lives during these times of need was "Old Man Guidi." Guidi owns a hole in the wall bar in Morgantown, West Virginia. He is the most kind-hearted man you will ever meet. He would have his bartenders drive him out to my parents' house, leave a care package and disappear. He never told us when he was coming and he never rang the doorbell. He brought yummy food as well as Snuggies for mom and I; they are those blankets that you actually wear by placing your arms through the sleeves and the blanket wraps around you backwards. If I went out for the mail and found a treat on our doorstep I knew it was from him. He was like the Easter Bunny or the Tooth Fairy.

April 23, 2009
Subject: Hahn update April 23

Hey Everyone!

Mom has had some tough days since last Thursday. During those days, she was told she was resistant to a drug treating an infection, had crazy low blood pressure, some swelling in her feet and ankles, and developed a suspicious rash. The doctors had her coming everyday as an outpatient.

HOWEVER, she is a new lady today!!!! We are on day 76 and she is kickin'!

They started Mom on a drug to increase her blood pressure to help with the black out episodes. It appears to be working, as we have had no issues since Easter Sunday. She had an infection they found in her urine and after a three day IV treatment has cleared it! Her swelling is getting better (caused by the blood pressure medicine), and her skin continues to heal. They are watching the new rash and treating it with steroids. They think it is a bit of Graft vs. Host Disease.

The good news is....since during the last two days her numbers were so good, they are going to give her Friday and Sunday off! Perfect timing since we are supposed to have a beautiful weekend here, sunny and 80 degrees. Also, we have been able to get Mom out for some lunches. This is so nice because she can feel somewhat normal. We have had some visitors in the evening and continue to have great helpers, my friends, fiancé and this past week, a friend of mom's from Ohio.

Lastly...a small request. My best friend Lisa is running her second marathon to raise money for leukemia. She is so dedicated and will be running in honor of my mom and a 21 yr old boy that we have become close with. Please check out her website. She wrote a nice piece on Mom and our friend Aaron. I know many of you made a donation for her first marathon in which she raised $3500. Thank you in advance for all of your support. http://pages.teamintraining.org/md/corps09/lgiove

Love to all!!!
Ash

My friend Lisa is amazing. She is this tiny little thing that can run forever. She too had a difficult battle, not with leukemia, but with anorexia. Lisa has turned her life around and is dating the man who she hopes will soon become her husband. This is the happiest I have ever seen her. She is eating much healthier and has completely beaten her battle.

Lisa is such a kind-hearted person. During Mom's battle, Lisa had signed up with Team in Training, an organization that helps raise money for research towards a cure for leukemia. Her website told an amazing story. Lisa ran for "Team Hahn." Two marathons later, Lisa had raised over $5000 that went to the Leukemia Foundation. She did an awesome job in the races and our family is thankful for her.

April 29, 2009
Subject: Hahn Update: April 29

Hello from the Hahn house, day +82 post transplant. We are rolling right along.

Here with a bit of good news!!! I believe back on day 75 mom made the turn! She has a strong, fighting attitude again and is ready to get better!!!

For example, yesterday, she put on makeup and her wig and called Dad to leave the office and meet for lunch. She also had a little fashion show in which she sat in a chair and tried on 20 plus garments that she had ordered online from February until now (even a bone marrow transplant couldn't stop this girl from shopping). She looked great in everything and we are now in search of some new bottoms since she has lost 30 pounds since the transplant. (Don't worry...its the 30 lbs she packed on before she went into the hospital)....although her legs are awfully small.

Her skin continues to heal and I told her by Friday she should be back to normal without Dad and me having to apply cream and cover it with pads. Thank goodness b/c this was very painful for several weeks.

Her appetite has improved and she still loves sweets. She is enjoying going to restaurants, feeling like a normal human being.

She is still 100% donor meaning the lady's marrow has replaced her immune system.

Lastly, Mom wants to do more on her own. Now that we have the black outs under control, she is able to walk with us by her side, not holding onto her. She takes an occasional arm if we are out and about because her legs are still very weak and rubbery....with time this will improve.

Love to all...keep praying....it's working!
Ash

Finally, I started to see "my mom" again. It was so nice to see her standing in the bathroom mirror applying makeup. Such a simple task we take for granted. It was not easy for her to get ready, but she felt great when she did. We loved eating at restaurants because it made Mom feel normal. It amazed me how all of a sudden she had made a positive turn around. I could not wait for day 100 to see how she would be then.

I kept mentioning the 100th day out from the transplant and how great it was supposed to be. At the 100-day mark, we would have a better indication of whether or not Mom's body had accepted or rejected the transplant. The doctors informed us that certain side effects, such as rashes, fever and uncontrolled nausea could be signs of rejection. Of course, we were praying we would not see any of them. The 100th day had been approaching. Nobody warned us of all the chaos we would face along the way, but we kept on trudging along, day by day, knocking out whatever we faced. Each day she was getting better.

CHAPTER 14: MAY 2009- WE REACH THE 100TH DAY

Boxer Jack Dempsey believed, "A champion is someone who gets up when he can't."

May 13, 2009
Subject: Hahn update: May 13

Hey everyone! Day plus 96 post-transplant.....Sunday is our BIG 100th Day!!!

Just a quick update....mom is doing well, continuing to get stronger each day, going on more outings, and capable of doing a tiny bit more around the house. She is also getting herself ready in the morning, including making her own breakfast and able to do the stairs in our house without our help. As the day goes on though, she tuckers out.

A couple things coming up to keep Mom in your thoughts and prayers. On Friday she will have another dreaded bone marrow biopsy. These are very unpleasant and she counts the seconds until they are over. On Monday, she will have her triple lumen line removed and an outpatient surgery to get a port put into her chest (another device they can use long-term to treat her/draw labs, etc).

Love to all. Hope everyone is enjoying the spring weather (minus all the rain!)
Ash

Who would have ever thought that two flights of stairs, consisting of 5 steps each, would be a struggle for my mom? As you can see in the previous email, she started doing them on her own. Not mentioned before, we would walk behind her on the stairs, often pushing her butt and praying she would get to the top without blacking out or getting too tired. Finally, she was on her own again. We laughed a lot because she would climb to the first landing, take a breather and then go the rest of the way. When she reached the last step, she would "stick the landing." She stood at the top of the staircase as if she had just climbed to the top of Mt. Everest. I am sure it felt like that every time for her. I couldn't be more proud of her for accomplishing the stairs. I know she hated feeling so helpless.

I want to mention how she had gotten some of her independence back. Before, Dad and I had to literally help dress her, roll a chair into the bathroom for her to sit on when she washed her face and brushed her teeth, prepare all of her meals, etc. For once, she felt as though she was the queen and everyone served her. Prior to being sick, she used to always do everything for us. When she was "really bad," I did not even let her take a step without me. I was so scared she would "go down on me." I followed her and held her arm everywhere she went, including the bathroom. I know she must have been so relieved when her blackouts subsided and I let her be free again. It is hard to pee with someone staring at you. :) Way to go Mom!

May 18, 2009
Subject: Hahn Update May 18: Post biopsy, post surgery

Day 101!!! Prayers answered, prayers needed. Mom got good news today. The test from the bone marrow biopsy came back and so far it looks good. The doctor had a smile on his face when he shared the news! We are soooo happy!!!!

Unfortunately, even with the good news today, Mom had a rough one. They removed her triple lumen and put a port in. The surgery went fine, however, they really had to dig around and her chest is extremely bruised, swollen and bleeding some. Our doctor from the Bone Marrow Unit is concerned with it getting infected because of how bad it looks. That's where more prayers come in. She is in pain, but has pain medicine she can take, and we will be icing it for the next several days.

I will sandwich the bad news with a bit more good. Our doc has approved us to go to the beach for Memorial Day weekend. So, Thursday after one last checkup, labs and any replacements, we will be off to

Bethany-Aunt Barbara's house. It will be great to be somewhere new and see our cousins and soak up the sun (minus Mom who must be under an umbrella at all times, but she can have her toes in the sand)!!!

Love to all,
Ash

Pictured below is Mom at Aunt Barbara's beach house.

My Aunt Barbara's beach house is amazing. It is located right on the beach in a private gated community in Bethany, Delaware. The place is absolutely gorgeous and whenever you go there, somehow you forget about your worries. It is very therapeutic. Maybe it is the view, or the 7 little ones running around, that make you forget your troubles. Yes, that's right, I said 7 little ones. My cousins Angie and Julie have 7 children between the two of them. They are the cutest little kids you have ever seen and it is so fun watching them run laps around the house or dig holes in the sand. They are free entertainment. They mean so much to me; I included all 7 of them in my wedding. I was so glad to get my mom to the beach. The beach was a success and Angie and Julie really helped out with Mom, giving Dad and I a nice break. This was our last little bit of time together, "just the three of us," before I had to head back to MD to complete a graduate course.

At this point, I had to take a summer graduate course back in Maryland or I would be removed from the program that I had started, and would be forced to reapply to the college. We were 100+ days out and I knew with Dad and a little help, I could do it. I would be traveling back and forth.

CHAPTER 15: JUNE 2009- SUMMERTIME

Country singer, Kenny Chesney has a line in one of his famous songs that says, "It's a smile, it's a kiss, it's a sip of wine…it's summertime!"

June 11, 2009
Subject: Hahn Update June 11

Hey everyone! I know you all missed me!!! Since my last email, I was in MD for ten days for two weddings and a grad course. While I was gone, Mom was with my dad, her friend Joni for two days, and many days on her own, yep, you read it right, home alone!!! It seemed like a LONG ten days. I think I was more worried about her than she was!!! I called several times a day to check in and make sure she was taking her pills, feeling ok, etc.

Mom did great and is improving each day. She is still going to the cancer center every Monday for labs and every Thursday for labs/doctor visits. She continues to take a ridiculous amount of pills, but they are weaning her off of them slowly. By the end of the day, she is exhausted!

When I was home on Monday, Mom and I ran errands. She walked through Target, Bed Bath and Beyond, and even went out to lunch! At home, she is cooking Dad some dinners, doing some laundry and even hitting the ironing board! Sometimes I think she does a little too much in a day, but she is eager to get back to a "normal" life.

She met with the doctor today. He took her steroid down again and told her that if her numbers continue to look good, that in a few weeks, he will cut her back to only going once a week to the cancer center.

I will continue to drive back and forth from WV to MD for a class Tues-Thurs, home in Morgantown, Fri. to Tues. My class ends the second week of July. Until my next update.....

Love to all!
Ash

I could not believe how much progress Mom had made in just ten days. It was unbelievable and very reassuring. She was forced to basically "grow up" and take care of herself. I was so proud of her walking through the stores with me. We used to joke that prior to her having this "energy" (I guess you could call it that?); she sat in the car like a "puppy dog" as I ran all of the errands. I did not want to leave her home alone, so I would bring her along in the car while I ran around. She would sit in the car with the cool air conditioning running, while I ran in and out of stores getting odds and ends. That day was different, we had actually turned the car off and Mom went in with me. She loved pushing the cart as it provided her a little extra security. I was very proud of her!

June 20, 2011
Subject: Quick Hahn Update June 20

Mom met with the doctor on Thursday. He took her down again on her steroids and even better, told her she will only have to go to the cancer center once a week now!!!! From living in the hospital, to being an outpatient everyday, to every other day, then three times a week, then twice a week, we never thought this day would come!!! She is such a trooper. Unbelievable!!!! We are so happy. Dad is by far the most fired up out of all of us!

On a little side note, Mom, Dad and my two girlfriends are taking me wedding dress shopping today! And, Dad has a b-day on Monday!!! Lastly, we are planning on hitting the beach for the 4th! Dad will leave from there for his 21 days on the road recruiting and I will be in WV a lot with Mom.

Love to all,
Ash

PS- We may need to get a hairdryer soon b/c mom is cha-cha-cha chia !!!!! Yep...her hair is SLOWLY growing!

First and foremost, the best news our family received after spending the majority of our time in and out of the hospital and cancer center, was the news that we would be going from our daily visits, to just once a week. That was a HUGE step! We were all pumped. Secondly, the wedding dress shopping…remember, Mom's main goal throughout this whole ordeal was to dance at my wedding. Well, in order to have a wedding, I had to go out and get a dress. My best friends, Heather, Lisa, my mom, dad and I went out to three stores. We laughed at how hideous some of the dresses looked and at the very last store had a little fun with Dad. We found the most outrageous dress anyone had ever seen and I put it on and told him how much I loved it. He just laughed and said it was…"fucking ugly." Apparently he knew it was all an act. We did end up finding my dress that day and we all absolutely loved it. I was so happy to have my mom there as I put on the dress and added a veil. We sent Dad out to get the car and Mom took out the checkbook. It was another huge expense, yet Mom was another step closer to fulfilling her dream. Lastly, two more things to celebrate: back to the beach for the 4th of July, and we were all excited about Mom growing her hair back. Woohoo!

We knew the whole process would be like a roller coaster, but after a trip to the beach and all of the ups, we were not ready for the steep hill down. How many ups and downs can you emotionally handle? We had to find a way to handle them though because they kept being thrown our way. We didn't have a choice. We knew Mom would continue fighting.

June 30, 2009
Subject: Important Hahn Update 6-30

Two steps forward, one step back. We need prayers!!! Mom is checking into the hospital today. Since the last update, she has not been able to eat very much. She had a lot of nausea and was just not feeling well. Today was her normal, weekly visit at the cancer center. A lot of her numbers from her labs were on the low side. Dr. Craig wants to admit her right now, until Friday or Saturday. Today they will perform a scope of her stomach which will be done down in the OR. They will have to stick a tube down her throat for this procedure. They will also begin to administer some drugs through her IV. They want to attack whatever it may be immediately. There are two possible causes of this right now. Dr. Craig is going to check for the CMV virus, which she had before, and is, treated through IV drugs, and/or test/monitor her for Graft Vs. Host Disease.

Dad was with Mom at the visit and asked the doctor if this is normal and how long it will last? The doctor said this is another part of the process. He is treating it aggressively and hopes once they get it under control that she will feel as good as she did before. She is being transferred as we speak from the cancer center to the 9th floor bone marrow unit.

Please continue to say prayers. I will send an update as soon as I have one.

Love to all,
Ash

I did not document anything between June 30th and July 5th, as I do not remember this short visit in the hospital. I think it is because I was in Maryland working on my graduate degree. The next chapter has the next email   I   sent.

CHAPTER 16: JULY 2009- MOM'S 42ND BIRTHDAY (WINK, WINK)

"We turn not older with years, but newer every day." –Emily Dickinson

July 5, 2009
Subject: Update 7-5

Thank goodness!!!!! Took Mom to the doctor today. After a very nauseous and blah weekend, we had some good news.

1. The biopsies they took of her stomach all came back normal :).

2. The CMV virus they are treating has dropped in half from sky high 149,000 in half to 62,000. It is a start...we want it to continue to trend down.

3. Her numbers looked good today. Her white blood cell count has soared back up from the shots. We even got to stop them a day early.

Other than that, she is still just eating small amounts; some meals are better than others. The plan is to stay on the same drugs she is on. He would like her to return to the cancer center on Thursday for labs and then she can have a week off. The doc saw her today and doesn't need to see her again until next Thursday. If all goes well, she will return back to her once a week visits.

Dad hits the road tomorrow....21 days in July spent recruiting. I finish my grad course this week and then will be back in WV the last 3 weeks of

July. Her friend and my cousin will be coming to stay with her this week while Dad and I are gone. Mom has a big day on Tuesday...her birthday!!!!

Love to all,

Ash

I felt like when I was away from Mom, was the time when all of the bad things happened. I am sure it was just a coincidence. It was so hard being away and not being by her side. I did not know how it would go with my dad being gone for 20 plus days in July. Yes, it would be a nice break from seeing her "bad days," but it would also be extremely hard since we had been through so much together. It was a long time to be separated. I was glad the timing of my course worked out and Mom would only be missing a week without Dad or I being there. Thanks again to Cher and Julie for helping at that time.

July 16, 2009
Subject: Hahn Update 7-16

Thank you all for Mom's birthday cards. We had a lot of fun opening them. I surprised Mom with lunch on her birthday with 9 of her friends. She had no idea when she walked into the restaurant that they would all be there, even some from Maryland and Ohio!

Prior to mom's birthday she had about 8 bad days. She had flu-like sluggish symptoms. No energy whatsoever, and she was not eating. Mom even got sick to her stomach a few of the days. It was just terrible. However, Tuesday was a turning point. She is feeling much better. Her energy level has increased (although she still tires out by the afternoon), and she is eating meals again. Woohoo!!!

Unfortunately, along with the good news comes some bad. Please start praying again, specifically for Mom's new immune system to kick in and fight off this CMV virus. I guess when Mom was in the hospital, they ran a test to see if she was resistant to the drugs they were giving her for this virus. She is!!! This is not good. Therefore, the two weeks of medicine she has been taking to fight against this disease has done nothing.

The doctor wants to wean her off of one of the anti-rejection drugs to see if she can fight this with her own new immune system. There is only about a 30% chance she can, so please, please, please pray for this to be the case!!! It will take several weeks to see if she is able to do this successfully.

If she is NOT able to fight this virus herself, then she will be admitted into the hospital for a couple of weeks for a very strong drug. She would receive this drug by IV every 8 hours. It would be a very difficult two weeks. We do not want to think about this, as this is option two. With prayers, we can skip this whole fiasco.....

Remember, Mom's donor was a 42-year-old lady. Therefore, come on lady....kick in, takeover, and beat this virus!!!!

Love to all,
Ash

July 27, 2009
Subject: Hahn Update 7-27

Hey everyone!

I know you all have been waiting patiently. Sorry this email is overdue and a bit lengthy. Since I last sent one on July 16th, Mom has weaned off of her one drug to try to kick her immune system into gear. We went to the doc today and last week's virus number went from 59,000 to 26,000. This was really good. He is going to continue to take her off her drug and we hope it continues to trend down. She had labs drawn today, but we will not know the number until later this week. Keep praying!

My Uncle Tim, Pat and little cousin Marc came to visit. We had fun and they helped out a few nights I had to go to MD. My dad is still out of town until the end of this week.

Mom has been doing a pretty good job. Eating more and sleeping well. Unfortunately, yesterday she scared me to death by having a little blackout. We were out to lunch at *Ruby Tuesdays*. It was so odd and out of nowhere. She hasn't had one since Easter! I knew we were seeing the doctor today and with the approval of a neighbor (previous bone marrow pharmacist), I did NOT take mom in. To my surprise, she recovered well. Got right up off the floor of the restaurant, ate some soup and walked to the car. She came home took a nap and even took a little walk outside.

The doc today thought it was due to dehydration. Her blood pressure was low, so he gave her a bag of fluids through her port. Hope it does the trick.

We ended our meeting with him by asking if he would approve a trip to Hilton Head, leaving next Monday, August 3rd. He thought it was definitely a possibility. We will see him Friday for one final look over and one last set of labs and if all goes well, we will be loading the car and driving south (yes, back to where this all began one year ago).

I will send a much shorter email on Friday letting everyone know the new CMV virus number and if we will be heading out!

Love to all,
Ash

Mom scared me to death in *Ruby Tuesdays*. Out of nowhere, she blacked out. As I said in the email, the last blackout had been on Easter. I was so scared and wanted to call 911, but my mom refused. We had an angel with us that day. The waiter in *Ruby Tuesdays* was a former military member and was so kind, as he helped calm me down. Yes me, because Mom was absolutely fine after she came back to. Literally, she was eating and teasing me immediately following the blackout. She started dancing in the booth and asked me," Why are you so worried? Look at me, I feel fine!" I could not believe it. Anyway, our angel walked Mom out, letting her hold his arm to the car, and told me to "take care of her." He was a young man, but very sweet, considerate and helpful. I was glad to have Mom back home from lunch and back to normal. I remember hoping that the blackout was just a fluke and that those episodes were not returning. I was scared again and knew I was home alone with her. I remember thinking that this better not become consistent or I would not be able to handle it.

July 31, 2011
Subject: Hahn Update 7-31

Beach Update:
We got the go ahead to pack up and hit the road!!! HOWEVER, plans have changed a little bit. After discussing the whole beach scenario, Mom, Dad and I decided that Hilton Head would be too far with a 10-hour ride and a whole lot of effort. We still WANT and NEED a vacation. My cousins, Ang and Jules saved the day. They are letting us use my Aunt Barbara's beach house in Bethany from Sunday until Thursday. This will be perfect!

Medical Update:
Mom's CMV virus level dropped a lot :) This time from 26,000 to 17,000. Again, a very good sign that her new immune system is fighting the

virus. We hope it continues to trend down.

Unfortunately, Mom has been REALLY weak and tired the last week. After reviewing our labs today, Dr. Craig realized she does not have any good white blood cells right now. Although her total count of white blood cells is at a decent level, only 6 % of them are "good cells." This means that only a tiny percent of her cells are the ones that fight infection and give her energy. This is a concern. Her new immune system and old immune system may be fighting one another. We have to wait and watch.

In the meantime, they gave Mom a shot today that lasts two weeks and should boost her white blood cell count, which in turn, should give her some strength back.

Prayers for good cells coming Mom's way AND for a fun, uneventful, trip to the beach!

Love to all,
Ash

Back to the beach. We should have known this was not a good idea. The beach is where we first got our dreaded news. Little did we know (remember mom was doing so much better) that this would be a beach trip that landed us back into the hospital. The first email in the next chapter will   explain   more.

CHAPTER 17: AUGUST 2009- ASH SAYS GOODBYE

"Love is missing someone whenever you're apart, but somehow feeling warm inside because you're close in heart." ~Kay Knudsen

August 7, 2009
Subject: Hahn Update 8-7

Mom has checked back into the hospital. We made it to Bethany Beach for a few days, but it didn't quite go as planned. Sunday when we got there, Mom was all right, just exhausted from the trip. Monday we got her down to the beach in the morning to sit under an umbrella and enjoy the sand and waves. When we went back up to the house, she needed both Brian and Dad to get her there. She was wobbly legged and borderline blackout mode. A doctor on the beach even ran over because she looked so weak. That afternoon she took a really long nap. Later that evening, she threw up and spiked a temperature. Tuesday and Wednesday she was feeling better, but completely drained. She would just lie on the couch all day. If she had to go anywhere, even the bathroom, one of us had to take her b/c she was so weak. Yesterday we drove home and Dad and I knew she had to go right in. He took her to the cancer center and they ended up admitting her into the hospital 9th floor. Her labs haven't shown anything, but she is still VERY weak, wobbly, and is not eating. She has a few bites and is done. They currently have her hooked up to fluids. They gave her one antibiotic. We are pretty much playing the waiting game. The docs will see her today and they have ordered a CT scan of her stomach. I will send an update again when I have more info.

Love to all,
Ash

One minute our toes were in the sand, the next minute we were in the hospital. Luckily, it was a very short visit. They pumped my mom with antibiotics and fluids and sent her on her way. Quick plug here for having health insurance. The bills that came to the house were astronomical. Thank goodness for Dad's insurance because the majority of each hospital stay, medicine, etc. was covered. Otherwise, my parents would not have been able to provide Mom with the treatment she needed. It is so important to have good health benefits.

August 9, 2009
Subject: Hahn Update 8-9

Hey everyone!

We are home again!!! They ran tests and checked labs and did not find anything. I am not sure why Mom got so weak and was feeling so bad.

In the hospital they gave her antibiotic via IV b/c of the temp she had spiked on vacation. They kept her on it all three days she was in there. Also, they pumped her with fluids.

She came home today and is eating much better. They upped her steroid by 35 mg. She is still a little wobbly, but I think it is b/c she hasn't been up and at 'em much the last few weeks. She will be getting a walker to help her do a little more exercising a day to rebuild her endurance.

We are on a desperate search to hire someone who can be with mom during the day while Dad is at work and for overnights when he has to travel. If anyone knows anyone, please let us know. I return to Maryland in one week....we are in a bit of a crunch.

Love to all,
Ash

I could not believe the time had come for me to return to Maryland, my fiancé, my job and my life. My amazing principal, Mr. Muhammad, had saved my position and I was fortunate enough to be going back to my same classroom, teammates and school. I thanked God for that privilege. I would at least be returning to what I was used to. As happy I was to be returning to what I was familiar with, I did not know how I was going to leave my parents. My mom had basically become my daughter and we were inseparable. I was petrified of letting go. I knew I had to though. We also knew that with his job, Dad could not do it alone. We had to begin interviewing someone to assist Mom throughout the day.

It was at this point when I went into freak out mode! I was going to leave what had become my day-to-day life and trust someone else to take my place. My OCD came out, and I started brainstorming a list of questions to ask people who were going to become my mom's caretaker. I also created a binder full of information and contact information for whomever we decided to hire. I was getting ready to trust someone else with Mom's life. Below is a one-page sheet that I had created for her helper.

The Hahn Household

Job Description: Companion, laundry (clothes, sheets, towels), ironing, preparation of meals, errands, trips to doctor's office, changing sheets once a week. Flexible hours, 4 or 5 hours a day, some overnights. Schedule planned each week based on doctor's appointments. We have a cleaning lady come once a week, so minimal housework, other than cleaning up in the kitchen and possibly watering plants.

Hours: Monday-Friday (4 hrs. a day) 11-3 except doctor days time TBA

Refill Mom's pill box for the week the day of her doctor's visit so if needed, you may stop by the pharmacy*

Mondays:
-Change Mom and Dad's sheets: Spare set is in the guest room closet on the left side next to the towels. You can make the bed with those and then wash the dirty ones and put them back into the closet. Thanks!
-Wash the "man room" pillowcases. The spare pillowcases are in the closet in the "man room."

Tuesdays:
-Errands

Wednesdays:
-Activity: Lunch, a movie, something to get her out of the house

Thursdays:
-Activity and/or errands

<u>Fridays:</u>
-Wash all towels in Mom and Dad's bathroom (including bath mats on the ground in there).

Very important

1. If Mom has an "episode," immediately get her to lie down, turn her head to the side and lift her legs up until she comes to. Keep saying her name. Call a neighbor and/or the first number on the purple folder. If she is not responding for a <u>long time</u>, call 911!!!

2. All necessary phone numbers of family, neighbors, and hospital are on the back of this

3. Mom must drink, drink, drink….at least 64 ounces a day. The WV cups in the cabinet are each 16 ounces. The juice cups are 6 ounces and the green coffee cups are 10 ounces.

4. Please walk with Mom wherever she needs to go. Bathroom, downstairs, upstairs, etc. ESPECIALLY pay attention on the stairs. Before she "takes off" anywhere, make her balance and remind her to keep her eyes up.
5. The white binder informs you of what to do if certain symptoms occur.

I now laugh at this document that I had created. It did not matter what day the person changed the sheets, what day the towels were washed, etc. As long as it got done, who cared? At the time, having it all written out made me feel better. I guess I felt as though I was "dummying down the directions." I did not want ANYTHING to be left out.

Also, Mom could kill me now looking back at her "fluid-intake." One of her main rules when she was discharged from the hospital was to drink a ton of fluids. The ounces I had come up with for the various glasses in the house were much lower than reality. For example, the 8-ounce cup I had given my mom 8 ounces of credit for was really 12 ounces. Accidentally, I had her drinking nearly double the amount she needed. Oh well! Maybe that had helped.

The last important item I mentioned above was in regard to the white binder. The white binder was our "Bible" that the hospital had sent home with us. Mom and I referred to it daily. It told us all of the information on the foods Mom was and was not allowed to eat, what activities she could do and when, which symptoms to just monitor, and when to call the doctors, etc.

I cannot believe I haven't mentioned it until now, but there were a ton of rules when Mom's counts were down. One rule was, everywhere she went she had to wear a mask. This was so she would not catch any germs from others. Also, her diet was very restricted. Everything had to be made fresh for her. She could not drink fountain sodas because of the bacteria, and she was never able to eat from a buffet, or anywhere else where food had been left out.

One of Mom's favorite places during her "bad times" was *Arby's*. For some reason, maybe it was the salt, she could taste an *Arby's* roast beef sandwich and craved them all of the time. I became friends with the employees at the *Arby's* in Morgantown. She often sent me over there from the hospital or cancer center to grab her lunch. It got to the point where from the moment I walked in, they had already knew what I was going to order, and even had a routine in place. The manager would inform his employees that my order was special. They would take their gloves off, re-wash their hands, place new gloves on and make her sandwich fresh from scratch. They would not put her food down the shoot or under the heat lamps; they would walk it around to me. In addition, they made fresh fries and placed them directly into the fry container for her. They went above and beyond. I was so impressed that I wrote to *Arby's* headquarters and reported the phenomenal experiences I had. The next time I went in, they thanked me for their recognition, and gave us a free lunch. There still are good people out there in this world who look out for others. Thank you *Arby's*!

There were far and few activities Mom was permitted to do when her counts were low. The binder had an entire list of what she was NOT allowed to do. These activities included gardening, swimming, horseback riding and much more. We laughed because Mom and I knew darn well she would not be gardening, she hadn't in years, and I could not imagine my mom on a horse. The only one of the activities listed above she was sad about was not being able to swim. However, we were not returning to a beach for a long time and her energy level would not allow for her to even step foot into a pool. It was good to know what was NOT allowed, but for once this did not affect us. Mom would tease me, telling me that once her counts were back, she was going to both garden and go horseback riding. Guess what? Two years out, she hasn't done either.

August 13, 2009
Subject: Important Hahn Update 8-13

A lot of information today, so bare with the longer email. Since mom has been out of the hospital she has been feeling good, eating and drinking, however, the second she stands up to walk anywhere, she is dizzy and wobbly. (She looks like she is drunk everywhere she goes).

Because of this, Dr. Craig wanted to perform two tests today, an MRI of the head and a spinal tap (removing fluid from the bone). The MRI was at 7:30 this morning. To our disappointment, they found two abnormalities on the brain. This is something to be VERY concerned about. There are three insights to these abnormal spots. First, and what we are PRAYING for is that there is an infection hiding. This would be the ideal situation and once they find out more about it, they could treat it with antibiotics. The second thing it may be would be leukemia in the brain. This would be treated by chemo into the head. I guess the transplant can fight leukemia cells in most of her body, however, the brain has a barricade up and it may be in there. The third, worst-case scenario would be that the spots show that mom had a stroke. If this is the case, there is not anything they could do for her other than physical therapy. Her dizziness and the way she feels would continue to get worst. He REALLY does not want this and at the same time is not suspecting that it is or was a stroke.

So, all those prayers praying NOT to get an infection need to be REVERSED. At this point in the course, we are praying that the abnormalities are due to an infection.

The spinal tap performed today will allow them to check for leukemia cells in the brain as well as to see if any bacteria/fungus grow which would show an infection. This could take days to weeks to find out the results.

We cannot believe this and are totally bummed, HOWEVER, we still have faith in our doc that he will treat whatever it may be. He says when you find out you have leukemia that you have a ton of battles to win before you can win the war. This is one more battle Mom has to overcome! He still said she would dance at my wedding, so she has to hurry her little butt up and get over whatever this bump is.

Lots of prayers are needed at this time. Oh, and by the way, after four interviews, we found someone we love. She is the girlfriend of one of the assistant coaches at WVU. I go to MD on Sunday and she begins helping Dad out on Monday.

Love to all,
Ash

It is so scary to think about anything regarding the brain. We were petrified, not to mention the timing could not be any worse with me returning to work. We knew with me returning to work that Dad could not be responsible for Mom alone. Anita lived just around the corner and was willing to help. This would work out well. I of course, left the whole binder of information regarding Mom's medications, my routines, and exactly what had to be done and on which days. Anita would check in on Mom, help her with some meals, get her prescriptions, go to her doctor appointments, etc. She would assume my role.

August 18, 2009
Subject: Hahn Update 8-18

Hey everyone! Greetings from MD! Just a quick note. Mom saw Dr. Craig today. All of the results came back negative; therefore, as of right now they are leaning towards the stroke. The doctor did not seem as concerned today as he had the first time he mentioned this possibility. He will be performing another spinal tap as well as another MRI within the next few weeks. She will also be receiving physical and occupational therapy at the house starting Monday. Hopefully this will allow her to regain some strength and provide her with strategies to try when she is feeling dizzy. Lastly, she will begin seeing some neurology docs. That is all for now...I will keep you posted as I get info. Dad is doing great and day one of Anita worked out well.

Love to all,
Ash

It is weird how one day the doctors can have you so freaked out about something and then turn around and make it seem like no big deal. Confusing to say the least. I remember being upset about the news, but also being reassured, because as I previously shared, I trusted and loved Dr. Craig. I knew if he was calm about the news, then I should have been too. I just worried about what was to come.

August 24, 2009
Subject: Hahn Update 8-24

Hey everybody!

I have officially been gone 7 days! Dad reported to me last night they had a great week! He has been a tremendous help, stepping it up every morning and every evening after work. Dad is not only back at work with his freshmen in town, but cooking and doing laundry. Thanks Dad!!!! Anita has been a great help too!!!

Medical update:

-Mom saw Dr. Craig today. Overall, her numbers looked good. Potassium was a little low, but they just gave her some extra by mouth.

-Mom had to have a repeat spinal tap today (always painful).

-They also are scheduling another MRI of the head sometime within the next few weeks.

-She will be meeting with the physical therapy people early this week.

-Mom is still dizzy...however, on a scale from 1-10, 10 being the worst, she said she has gone from a 10 to 8.5. I hope it continues to improve!

-She is doing a bit more (not sure Dad and I approve) on her own now.

-Her vision is blurred, but when she told the doc today he did not seem too concerned...guess it goes with everything else.

I will email again when I know more!
Love to all,
Ash

PS-Mom checks emails again, so if you want to send her a note her address is _____ or you can reply to this......

I always forward her any responses. Thanks!

Dad was amazing throughout everything and he still continues to amaze me to this day. I cannot imagine watching a spouse suffer like that. Nonetheless, he remained upbeat, and continued to push Mom along. Not only was he worried about her, but he also had a job he had to focus on. Even though Dad had to work full-time, he still helped out from the minute he got home, until he went to bed. He even did as much as he could in the morning before he left for the office. Not only did he perform his duties as an assistant basketball coach, he had a full-time job at home helping Mom and I out. My dad is the toughest, most faithful man I have ever met. Mom and I are forever grateful for him.

Mom, as previously mentioned, had probably been doing a little more than Dad and I approved of. Even though Dad was there a lot to help, she still was her own self-reliant woman who took care of the house when he was at work. I clearly remember one day my fiancé and I going to the house and wondering how the light out front was shining bright. It had been burnt out for a while and nobody had paused his or her busy schedules to replace it. Well, I asked my mom, "Who changed the bulb out front?" She looked around the room sheepishly, and then turned to Brian and smiled and said, "I did. All by myself." My fiancé and I looked at each other in disbelief. Yes she did. One day when home alone, she drug a stepladder outside, stood up on it and changed the light bulb. Keep in mind, her vision was blurry and she still occasionally felt dizzy. I could not believe it. I scolded her and immediately called my dad to tell him what she had done. We watched her like a hawk from then on.

August 29, 2009
Subject: Hahn Update 8-29

Hey everybody,

Just a brief update from last week. Mom saw a neurologist. He read the past MRI to her and said, "I don't really see anything to be concerned about." The spots on the brain were very tiny, in fact Mom and Anita could barely see them without them being pointed out. He was not convinced though that she did not have an infection, so he sent her off for more labs and cultures. She is doing a bit more each day, making her own breakfast, going up and down stairs alone again, etc. Anita has gotten Mom out to lunch twice in the past week :) She is eating great now and hopefully the physical therapy will help build her strength back. A spinal tap was performed last week and a repeat MRI will be done. She will also be sent to another specialist. Her vision in her left eye is still pretty bad and she is still dizzy (although she has gone from a ten, ten being the worst to a 7.5). Mom, Dad and everyone just want this to all be done and her to be better! She has had enough!!!!!!!!!!!!!!!!!!!!

Love to all,
Ash

It was hard not being there for the appointments anymore. I wanted to be by my mom's side but I couldn't. I had to trust Anita to be her advocate and help speak up for her at the appointments. I also had to trust that she would keep her company and keep her spirits lifted. Mom was hitting a breaking   point   and   so   were   Dad   and   I.

CHAPTER 18: SEPTEMBER 2009- A VISIT TO WV

Mother Theresa expressed, "Love begins by taking care of the closest ones - the ones at home."

Mom has always been a die hard catholic. She attends church every Sunday, prays every night before bed, and says the Rosary to feel better during trying times. I was headed home, to take care of my mom, even if it was for a short time.

September 3, 2009
Subject: Hahn Update Good News 9-3

Awesome news this week!!!! After a rough start on Sunday when Mom took a spill and cut her head (she had to be glued and has two huge black eyes from it), the week turned around for the better! Mom had a doctor appointment early in the week, a visit with the physical therapist and an eye doctor appointment ALL with GREAT news!!!! :)

-Dr. Craig said she is doing well. Her CT looked good, spinal tap was normal and he was pleased with her numbers. She has been given permission to get off that special diet, and is able to eat anything she wants again including a glass of wine!!! He thinks as he lowers her meds, that her dizziness may decrease.

-The physical therapist thought Mom was doing great and just wants to do a few sessions of arm and leg exercises to help her gain some strength back.

-The eye doctor said she has swelling in her left eye and the start of a cataract, which can be fixed with special lenses if all, goes well. She will see him again in four weeks.

Lastly, due to all of the good news this week, Mom's attitude has taken a turn for the better. She is the happiest Dad has seen her in a long time. She is perkier on the phone and has been making some meals for Dad and herself.

Hope everyone is doing well. We are happy at the Hahn household!

Love to all,
Ash

It's amazing how life works out. Mom, Dad and I had been feeling "down" and then we got the good news. Someone was looking out from up above. I want to touch on the part from the email when I say Mom took a spill, hit her head, ended up glued shut and received two black eyes. Mom, the overachiever, decided she was going to start dinner by herself and went out to the garage where she kept a Crockpot. Well, on her way back in, she tripped on a step and fell, dropped the Crockpot and hit her head. Thank God for amazing neighbors. She called down the street to her friend Barbie and her husband who happens to be a general practitioner. Barbie and Brian rushed down to help Mom. Brian got glue from his office nearby and took care of Mom's head, and Barbie helped clean up the glass from the lid of the Crockpot. We had the best neighbors through all of this. We cannot thank them enough for always being on call. Mom was embarrassed, yet I was so proud of her for calling them. I felt so bad because she was only trying to surprise my dad. She wanted to have dinner prepared for him, but it ended up backfiring. A simple task went totally wrong.

September 17, 2009
Subject: Hahn Update 9-17

Two more great weeks!!! Since I last sent an email, Mom has continued to get good news.

-She met with an infection disease specialist who did not see any problems in any of the tests/results

-Dr. Craig has taken her down to visits every other week....she is really looking forward to her weeks off of appointments

-Her physical therapist said her strength has improved 70% and has dismissed her from the rest of her sessions

Lastly, they want to do another MRI just to make sure things are alright and to get a picture of the eye that is still bothering her.

Mom's spirits are up and she continues to do more and more everyday!!!

Keep the prayers coming. Things are lookin up!!!

Love to all,
Ash

September 29, 2009
Subject: Hahn Update Sept. 29

Hey everyone!

I FINALLY got home after being away for a month (seemed like sooo much longer). Mom looked great!!! I was pleasantly surprised with what a turn she has made the last few weeks. Since when I left her, she is really up and moving, walking the stairs much better, able to get out and about some, and was able to cook her own dinner :) It was wonderful to see her having some independence back and strength. Her attitude it great!!!

The ONLY thing bothering Mom/holding her back some from her normal activities are her eyes. They are swollen and her left eye is barely open and waters ALL the time. The docs referred her to a cataract specialist/eye surgeon. She saw him on Monday. He told us that it could be one of three things and that he wants to do some further testing. One it could be some leukemia cells in the eye, which they could remove with surgery. The second reason could be due to the amount and strength of meds she is on and the third a possible infection. He could see that layers of her eye had torn. He was pleased though that new layers were developing (I wonder if this is like the skin and fingernails she lost...maybe this is another part of the body the lady takes over!?)

Please continue to pray for Mom...she needs to see again!!!

Love to all,
Ash

I remember my first trip back to West Virginia. I could not wait to see my mom and dad. I was shocked at how much progress Mom had made; yet it was still so sad to see her dealing with the ongoing side effects. I wondered, when was it ever going to end? I helped as much as I could in my short visit. I remember that the goodbye was super hard at the end of the weekend. Mom, Dad and I all cried. It felt good though to finally let some emotions out.

CHAPTER 19: OCTOBER 2009- EYE TROUBLE

"The question is not what you look at, but what you see." –Henry David Thoreau

October 1, 2009
Subject: Update-oh man :(

So..............Mom saw Dr. Craig today and he wants to admit her into the hospital tomorrow for a week. Although her counts all look good, and she feels good, he is concerned about her eyes and vision. After consulting, the eye doctor and Dr. Craig both think the likely cause of her blurry vision is the CMV virus of the eyes. They will begin treating it with a drug via IV. Mom needs to stay in the hospital b/c the drug will knock her calcium, potassium, etc counts down and she will be needing replacements. Please pray for a speedy recovery and that the meds work!!!! She will have her laptop and her cell if you want to be in touch. Again, she feels fine and is very strong, she just can't see!!!

Love to all,
Ash

I remember when Mom got the news that day. It made absolutely no sense to any of us. She had felt fine and her numbers were good, so it was hard for her to imagine having to check back into the hospital for her eyes. We hoped it would only be a short visit. Dad shared with me that she sat in the chair at the hospital a lot more than the bed. Mom wasn't feeling sick and didn't feel like she belonged there.

October 6, 2009

Subject: Hahn Update 10-6

Mom got out of the hospital last night earlier than expected!!! She will have to go in as an outpatient to the cancer center for the next several weeks. They will administer the drug there and every night she will give it to herself at home. I will send an update when I know more....some people have asked for Mom's email address and phone number.

Email: _____
cell:_____

Big Hugs!!!
Ash

There she went again, overachieving. The doctors said a full week, and she got out in five days. Even though she had to go to the cancer center everyday, she felt like she had so much more freedom than when she was sitting in the hospital. Although the cancer center took hours, she at least knew sooner than later, she would be sitting on her own couch or lying in her own bed. Every cancer center visit had an end in sight.

October 12, 2009
Subject: Hahn Update: 10-9

Just a quick update. Mom has not noticed any change in her eye sight yet (they said it could be weeks), HOWEVER, a specialist looked at them today and he did see some improvement :) Hopefully it continues to get better. She is still going into the cancer center daily to receive the drug and administers it to herself every night.

Mom got a surprise on Thursday. Matt flew home for a long weekend :) She enjoyed spending time with him.

Dad has been staying busy with workouts, recruiting and helping Mom with appointments, around the house and cooking some dinners...he has done a wonderful job. Last week he surprised me by stopping by my classroom (he had a funeral he had to attend at University of Maryland). Good ole Bill walked into my classroom with a pumpkin mask!!! The kids just sat there staring trying to guess who the "pumpkin man" was :)

Hugs to all,

Ash

Another prime example of my dad being a great man. As busy as he was recruiting in Maryland, he took time out of his day to swing by my classroom for ten minutes to say hi to me and see my class. He has always been a practical prankster and loves to tell jokes. Well, I am not going to lie when I say, he scared the crap out of me that day when he walked into my room with a pumpkin mask on. I tried to be brave for the kids, but I was thinking, "Who is this freak?" LOL :) It only took me a minute before I knew just who it was. The students loved meeting my dad.

My class was very special during my first year back to teaching after taking Family Medical Leave. They were so worried about my mom because I often told them how I took care of her and how she was getting better. They also loved my family picture I had sitting on my desk. My class made several cards for her and anytime I went home to visit, they sent their love with me. They were a sweet group. I definitely had needed a nice class that year.

October 19, 2009
Subject: Hahn Update Oct. 19

Hey everyone!

Bri and I went to spend the weekend with Mom and Dad. Very briefly, dad is doing great...we saw Mountaineer Madness and he kicked off his first practice of the season. They look good!!!

Mom continues to do well, although says she is still having trouble seeing. I do NOT notice her squinting as much though which I think is a good sign. We were able to get out to lunch and have some fun. She met with Dr. Craig today and he sent her back to going into the cancer center Monday, Wednesday and Friday for her drug. The other days she will administer it to herself at home. She has two more weeks of this drug and then hopefully she will be able to see better. I was very excited to see she had a letter from her donor...please see below....

PS- I did some detective work and found out the lady writes to us in German!!! You see, the transplant coordinators cross all information out with a black permanent marker on the cards, but I held it up to the light and read it :) I am copying the letter word for word from the one Mom received.

Love to all,
Ash

<u>*Another letter from the Donor:*</u>
Dear ....,

At first I a big "sorry" that I write you so late and I write in German (crossed off, but I read it), but in the last months we had a lot to do with managing things in the right way. We had to sell my house (a lot to tidy up) and then my big daughter was sad, she burden herself with the separation, house selling and and and....

Well, thank you very much for your nice card, it is nice to know more about you and I hope you are doing well. Are you still in hospital? What about the marriage?

I found this card, and I had the feeling that it fits to us.

Maybe you can write in America you are from, it is quite difficult to make a picture from you and one wants to know so much. With best wishes, and I hope to hear from you.

Card:
Wherever your way goes along
A guardian angel should be with you
At the morning with sunrise
At night when the stars glow
And in every hour of your life.

It was always so nice receiving letters from our donor. Since there was a language barrier, some of it was confusing, however, you still get the gist of what a beautiful, thoughtful, lady Mom's donor was. The card she picked out was so special and so was the donor!

October 28, 2009
Subject: Short Hahn Update

Mom met with an eye specialist today. Although Mom does not see any improvement with her vision, he still does. He has seen a 60% change. I think this is great news. He told Mom that he cannot promise it will come back, but for the time being, we are happy.

Love to all,
Ash

Mom's eye specialist was amazing. Dr. Jabbour was very kind and was really good at his job. He took time to meet with his patients and explained in detail their diagnosis, as well as his detailed plan of action. He really bonded with our family and treated us well. People traveled for hours to come see him. He was a miracle worker and we hoped he could help Mom.

CHAPTER 20: NOVEMBER 2009- BACK IN THE STANDS

There is a Japanese Proverb that says, "Fall seven times, stand up eight."

Although Mom was put on her butt several times, in November of 2009, she stood back up in the stands at Dad's game. Instead of him cheering her on, she resumed her role of being his number one cheerleader.

November 4, 2009
Subject: Hahn Update Good News 11-4

Hey everyone!!!

Great news!!!!!!! Mom saw Dr. Craig today and everything is going well again. She did not need any replacements and her numbers looked great. She is doing so well that he is giving her two weeks off! This is her first break from appointments in over a month. She is ecstatic! Dad had a day off from practice today, so they used a gift certificate we got them way back in June for their anniversary to go out to a fancy dinner!!! Perfect timing to celebrate the good news and actually be on a date again :)

Big hugs!!!
Ash

November 11, 2009
Subject: Hahn Update 11-11

Mom saw eye specialist today:

-after his tests he saw "marked improvements"
-the thing that was eating her eyes (virus) is gone
-the blurriness she is seeing is scar tissue...should go away
-he was so pleased; he does not want to see her for a month

She will still see Dr. Craig every two weeks. Last weekend, she got to Dad's exhibition game and went out after for wings and a beer!!! She stayed out until around 10 pm and is hoping to do a repeat this Sunday when Dad plays Loyola!

Love to all,
Ash

I was so happy to hear that Mom was getting to my dad's basketball games again. It was a great feeling knowing that Mom was getting back to normal. And, even better news that she went out to celebrate afterward. She even had a beer! Maybe the grueling battle was finally coming to an end.

CHAPTER 21: DECEMBER 2009- HOLIDAYS TO CELEBRATE

"Gifts of time and love are surely the basic ingredients of a truly merry Christmas." - Peg Bracken

December 13, 2009
Subject: Hahn Update 12-13

Hey everyone...bet you missed me :)

Mom has been doing well. The other day she went to the mall for an hour, out to lunch, Dad's game, and out for a beer after....days are becoming more normal!!! We are thrilled.

Unfortunately, her eyes are still a problem. Apparently in her one eye, her retina is detaching. The eye specialist has decided to do an outpatient surgery. She is scheduled for Thursday, however, has an appointment tomorrow (Monday) to see if it needs to be sooner. If he sees there is a need to do it right away, he will perform surgery tomorrow night (Monday). Please say a prayer that all goes well and it solves the problem!

In closing, Mom is excited about the holidays. Matt will be able to get home the 21st-24th and I will head home on Christmas for a full week (gotta love teaching and winter breaks!)

Big hugs!
Ash

December 17, 2009
Subject: Surgery

Mom's surgery was this morning. It was an outpatient surgery. She was uncomfortable during it, but not in any pain. The doctor thinks all went well and will see her first thing tomorrow morning to hopefully remove the patch. I talked to her several times today and everything seems alright :)

I will send a short email once she hears from the doc tomorrow.

Ash

December 22, 2009
Subject: Hahn Update Good News For the Holidays

Mom saw Dr. Craig today and the eye specialist and received good news and even better news. Dr. Craig said all of her numbers looked good and that he doesn't need to see her for another month. At that time, he will start giving her child immunizations. Yes you read it correctly, she will have to start getting all of the childhood shots..polio, pox, influenza, hep etc. They will do a few every 3 months for awhile. This is normal once someone hits the year mark and she is almost there (Feb 6th).

After Dr. Craig, we went over to the eye specialist and Mom said to him, "I just got good news at the cancer center so keep it coming." Her doctor said, "I have even better news for you...your vision is four times better than it was on Friday." (as in 3 days ago!) He told her things were looking good...she can go down on her eye drops and he will check again in a week

Happy Holidays to all!!! The Hahn family has a lot to be thankful for....Thanks again for all your prayers and support over the last year....Mom really thinks everyone has helped her through this :)

Cheers to a happy, healthy 2010 and hopefully a WVU National Championship!!!

Love to all
The Hahns

That holiday was extra special for us. We were home as a family and we had a lot to celebrate. Mom actually felt normal again and we enjoyed our time together. I will never forget that Christmas. I knew everything everyone was getting from Santa, because that year I was Santa. I had used Mom's credit card and got everyone's gifts for her. I guess you could call me Santa's Little Helper. I loved doing it. She felt so bad that I shopped for my own gifts that year, but it didn't matter to me. I was so happy that she was doing well. My parents ended up surprising me that Christmas with one of my mom's diamond tennis bracelets. I guess I didn't quite know ALL of the gifts. It was gorgeous and still to this day, I keep it in a safe unless I am going to a fancy event. Christmas 2009 was a good one! Mom appeared to be on the upside of things.

December 30, 2009
Subject: Hahn Update Dec. 30

I took Mom to the eye specialist yesterday for another follow-up to her surgery. Dr. Jabbour had more great news for her. He told us she has "phenomenal" vision and that she can drop her eye drops down to twice a day. He also thought she was doing so well that he would wait to see her in two weeks. It sounds awesome, but Mom still can't see a thing, so hopefully what he is seeing will soon be the case for Mom....she just wants to see again and be able to drive!

Love to all and Happy New Year!!!
Ash

Mom described her sight as "looking through wax paper." Dr. Jabbour thought it all looked good, but my mom was still blind. The thought of having her drive herself places sooner than later had made me uneasy. How would she get herself around if she could only see out of one eye?

CHAPTER 22: JANUARY 2010- A NEW YEAR

Charles Lamb stated, "New Year's Day is every man's birthday."

January 15, 2010
Subject: Hahn Update January 15

Hey everyone!
Mom saw her eye specialist today. Unfortunately, he saw "gunk" in her eye. He will need to perform another surgery sooner than later b/c the "gunk" is putting pressure on the buckle he gave her in the previous surgery. He could not believe that Mom could even see at all out of that eye with all of the "gunk" in it.

Hopefully, this will be the answer! Sorry for the silly lingo, but that is the word he kept using. Please pray for Mom on Thursday. It is an outpatient procedure.

Other than this, she is doing well. She is home alone a lot, making her own meals, and getting around fine when she has the opportunity to.

A big thanks to neighbors and friends who have been getting Mom out and about for lunches, appointments, etc!

Big hugs!
Ash

Two surgeries on one eye all in less than a month. That is a lot for anyone, let alone someone who has been through the ringer. She knew she had to do it though, so back she went for round 2. At least we trusted Dr.

Jabbour, so that was reassuring. Did you know for eye surgery you are awake and they just numb the eye? That part freaked Mom out. She could not stand the noises and how it felt. She shared that is was not extremely painful but it was not very comfortable either, and overall was very scary.

January 21, 2010
Subject: Hahn update Surgery Jan 21

Good morning!
Mom is already out of surgery. I have talked to her twice. This surgery was more painful than the last, but the doctor thought it went well. She seems to be doing fine and is already on her way home to rest. There are two follow up appointments scheduled, one for tomorrow and another for Monday. I will send a brief update after Mondays'. Thanks for all the prayers!

Big Hugs!
Ash

January 25, 2010
Subject: Short Hahn Update 1-25

Mom saw the eye specialist today. She was pleased with the news. He said the retina is still attached and looks good. Also, he sent some tissue away for some further testing and the results came back "clean." He is giving her one-week off. Hopefully things continue to heal.

Lastly, Mom will see her main doctor, Dr. Craig, on Wednesday for her first appointment since before x-mas! I will send you a little note after that.

Big Hugs!
Ash

January 27, 2010
Subject: Hahn Update 1-27 Post Doctor

Mom saw her main doctor today (Dr. Craig). All GREAT news :)

Her numbers looked good. She has over a month before she sees him again on March 8th and he even cut down one of her pills :)

She was thrilled....let's just hope the eye settles and then she will be feeling REALLY good :)

Her next steps are continued eye doctor appointments and at the beginning of March, see Dr. Craig for her first round of shots. Yep..that's right! She has to go through all of the vaccines you take as a child again! Her first appointment, she will have 6!!! UGH.....but other than that she is good to go :)

BIG HUGS!
Ash

January of 2010 was busy with surgery. The next month marked the big one-year anniversary. We were all hoping that the one-year milestone would mean NO MORE issues. Little did we know there would still be more   to   come.

CHAPTER 23: FEBRUARY 2010- HAPPY 1ST BIRTHDAY MOM

Pablo Picasso expressed, "It takes a long time to become young."

So, they tell you one good thing about getting a transplant is the fact that you then have two birthdays to celebrate each year. Your real birthday and your transplant date. A patient's transplant date is an extra special day to celebrate the day they were given a new life. Mom's was quickly approaching.

February 1, 2010
Subject: Hahn 2-1-10 The Big Day Is Approaching

Hey everyone!

Just wanted to send an email to share some more happy news. Mom saw the eye doctor today and although she says she can't see, she was able to read several letters for him. He even started off big and continued to make them smaller. She did well. He has given her two weeks off before he checks again.

BUT....our BIGGEST NEWS IS

Drum roll.....

Mom's ONE-YEAR ANNIVERSARY is this Saturday!!! One year ago, February 6th, she had her transplant!!! She has come a long way and Dad, Matt and I are so proud of her for fighting this hard. We have a lot to celebrate!!! She kicked cancer number 2's ass!!! Pardon the French :)

HUGE HUGS TO ALL!!!!!
Ash

Mom's first birthday! We never thought that day would come. It seemed so far off at the time, but it was finally here! As I shared in the email above, we could not have been happier for Mom. She did it again. She overachieved. Mom got so many "first birthday" cards. It really made us smile.

February 17, 2010
Subject: Hahn Update 2-17 ugh!

Thank you for all of the cards, phone calls, emails and gifts for Mom's one-year celebration!

Unfortunately Mom's eye appointment did not go well today. She is going in tomorrow morning for another surgery. The doc explained that a retina can be like an old t-shirt and if you mend one spot, another might start to have problems....he wants to go in the same eye and fix the other side of it. Her surgery is at 9:30 in the morning. Again, he is staying positive and thinks that this will do it.

Please say some prayers! Any thoughts or words to lift her spirits are much appreciated!!!

Big hugs!
Ash

Are you kidding? Coming off the high of the one-year post transplant celebration, and Mom got kicked in the gut again. A third surgery on the same dang eye. It was getting old. Mom was down. When would the punches quit being thrown?

February 20, 2010
Subject: Hahn update 2-20

Mom's surgery went well. She had a follow-up appointment yesterday and he was pleased with what he had done. Unfortunately, her eye is swollen shut right now, but when she called to ask them if it is normal, they said it was a good sign and showed them that she was keeping her head down as she was told to.

Her friend Cher, Brian and I are here today to take her to Dad's game and out after to celebrate the big one-year that got postponed due to the snowmaggedon we had in Maryland. She won't be able to see what she is doing but she will enjoy it:

Big hugs!!!
Ash

At least all three surgeries went well and Mom did not have any complications. Remember, always look for the positive side of things and stay upbeat. Although a little late, Brian, Cher, Mom and I got to celebrate. We were so proud of her.

CHAPTER 24: MARCH 2010- NCAA TOURNEY WATCH OUT

Former West Virginia Mountaineer basketball player Jerry West once said, "You can't get much done in life if you only work on the days when you feel good."

If Mom chose not to "work" on days she wasn't feeling good, then she would not be where she is today. And that March, she worked hard to be able to go to the tournament to cheer her boys on.

March 3, 2010
Subject: Hahn update 3-3

Mom saw the eye specialist. She got good news. Her pressure looked good, her bubble looked good, he lowered the amount of drops she is getting and she has a whole week off!

Keep your fingers crossed for Monday...appointment with the big guy, Dr. Craig!!! She will probably be starting her baby vaccines that day :(

Big hugs!
Ash

We really wanted good news. March Madness had begun and both boys had a chance at going to the NCAA tournament. My dad's team, West Virginia, looked promising and my brother's team, Vermont, had a good shot of winning their conference tournament, which would guarantee them a spot at the "Big Dance." We really wanted Mom to get approval to travel to whatever site Dad was placed so she could watch some hoops. We REALLY hoped that both boys would get in and that they would land in the same city. Highly unlikely, but hey, still worth having our fingers crossed.

March 15, 2010
Subject: Hahn Update 3-15

For those of you who don't know, both Matt and Dad won their championships on Saturday!!! :) It was an awesome weekend for the Hahn family. Sunday brought even better news..Matt's team, VT will be facing Syracuse in Buffalo, NY, and WVU is going up against Morgan St. also in Buffalo. So...the whole family will be together at the first round of the NCAA tourni!!!

Today, Mom got good news. She saw the eye doctor who again was pleased with what he saw and said her eyesight is improving. She even told me today that she could read the test better :) He is giving her 3 weeks off until he checks again....hopefully, she makes a lot of progress between now and then.

Mom plans to travel with the team. I will be meeting her, Matt and Dad on Friday :) Can't wait to have the whole family together!!!! We have a lot to celebrate!!!!

Could 2010 be the yr for the Hahns?!

Big Hugs to all!!!
Ash

We could not have been happier for the boys. There are so many sites where the tournament is played at, that we had really lucked out to be placed in the same region. Dad was excited that Mom and I could go and Matt was thrilled to have little Vermont at the biggest basketball tournament of the year. Articles were written in the New York Times, as well as some other newspapers, about the Hahn boys both coaching in the 2010 NCAA tournament. Those articles also included Mom and her amazing story. Unfortunately, Matt lost in the first round, but Dad's team went on and made it to the Final Four! However, the season came to a dramatic end when their star player went down during the final moments of the game. The Eers just could not pull off that win to head to the championship game. It was an amazing season anyway and an amazing time together for our family. The question was; was this the year of the

Hahn's? Had our luck changed? My wedding was quickly approaching and it looked promising that Mom would be there dancing.

Mom's road was just beginning.

CHAPTER 25: MAY 2010- MY BIG DAY

John Lennon and Paul McCartney sang, "All you need is love."

May 5, 2010
Subject: Hahn Update May 5

Hey everyone!

I am sure you have missed me :) Mom is doing great! She came to MD last weekend for my bridal shower and was a champ. Her energy level is definitely rising and she is getting out to do more and more each week. She went to Dr. Craig's office today and got great news. Her numbers all looked good and they decided not to start any vaccines for a while until he takes her off a steroid she is still on. Also, she is right on track and they have given her 2 months off!!! That's right....2 months :) Her next appointment at the cancer center will be in July :) She said a yr ago, she would be dancing at my wedding and she definitely will be....24 days and counting! We will be sure to post pictures for all!!!!!

Big Hugs!!! Thanks for the continued prayers.

Ash

It was awesome having my mom at my bridal shower. I could not have been happier that she was able to make the trip to Maryland to be with me. It was so nice opening presents and playing games, while glancing up and seeing my mom's smiling face. She looked so pretty too, just sitting there on the couch by my side as we ooed and awed over the gifts. It was a special day because not only were people very happy for me with my big day approaching, but also they were thrilled to see my mom out and about. For many of our friends and family at the shower, that was the first time they had seen her since her battle had begun. I was ecstatic each time someone whispered in my ear, "Your mom looks amazing." "She's doing great." I smiled as any proud "mother" would. Mom smiled back, proud to have me as her daughter.

May 12, 2010
Subject: Hahn Update May 12

Mom saw her eye specialist today. He told her she is a miracle. Her eye is as good as it could be. He doesn't want to take credit for it, so he said that it must have been God. Compared to where she was, her eye being eaten away by that virus, and now, he can't believe how good it looks. She can still NOT see, but he likes what he sees on his end. Dr. J even gave Mom 6 weeks off, but due to his vacation, her appointment is in a month so he can see her before he leaves.

Then, to make the day even better....Mom got a call from the bone marrow unit transplant coordinator. She has been nominated by them to meet her donor at the national bone marrow convention held this summer in Minnesota.....I hope she is chosen because that would be an AMAZING day for us :)

Again, thanks for all of the prayers. And, a huge thanks to the neighbor ladies and Morgantown friends who have been helping Mom so much. Dad has also been awesome and spending all his free time with Mom even if it is running errands or going to the doc!

Big hugs to all!
Ash

As I write this book, I know Mom was not chosen to meet her donor at that convention. We were hopeful, but someone else was given that special opportunity. Mom continues to email her donor and I know one day they will meet face to face.

The nomination was an honor and the kind words the transplant coordinator wrote about my mom were extremely special. As much as the doctors and nurses touched our lives, I think the Hahn family also touched theirs. We had a special bond with everyone who became part of Team Hahn. Below, is an excerpt of the application they had sent in.

[***Question 2: Besides the desire to have the donor and recipient meet,

118

what circumstances and/or information makes your nomination unique or special?

***Kathi's enthusiasm for life uplifts our staff and inspires everyone she meets.

After surviving ovarian cancer, she was diagnosed with ALL and immediately

began high dose chemotherapy. After remission was achieved and a donor was

identified she was admitted to begin the long process of matched unrelated allogenic HPC transplant. Kathi's fondest memory of the transplant process was her first day on the unit during rounds. The BMT team entered her room and her husband, Coach Hahn stated, "If you're not in it to win, then get out.".........the entire team remained. She understood that everyone was committed to her success as she and her family were.

Coach Hahn used his skills to continuously motivate and encourage Kathi and everyone on the BMT unit. During a donor drive in the Spring of 2009, he recruited many of his players to become donors. He also made himself available during the drive to answer questions regarding his personal experience of the transplant process. Every patient and transplant team could benefit from "Coach Hahn."

Her daughter, Ashley, postponed her wedding and relocated to Morgantown to act as her mom's full-time caregiver throughout the transplant and recovery process. The long anticipated wedding is now scheduled for May 29th of this year. Kathi is passionately involved in making her daughter's wedding a dream come true. Her joy radiates from her eyes and her smile is infectious. We are excited for Kathi, Ashley and the entire family. Kathi has promised to share Ashley's wedding day with us through pictures.

As mentioned above, Kathi is the wife of one of the assistant basketball coaches of WVU and is an avid fan. If you follow college basketball at all you have heard of the success the WVU team had over the last three years. Kathi was unable to attend many of the games during her treatments, transplant and recovery. This year she was able to return to the stands to witness the Big East Tournament for the first time ever. Her son and husband are both coaches and had teams in the opening round of the NCAA tournament. The entire Hahn family was able to be there together. Her journey was documented in The New York Times, The Washington Post, and ESPN. The mother of one of the players on her son's basketball team was going through treatments for cancer. The families bonded and supported each other through the journey. The articles were published the week of the tournament.

Kathi and her donor have corresponded anonymously from day one and the strong bond between them has grown over the last year. Kathi wants nothing more than to meet the woman who unselfishly gave her a second chance at life and to personally thank her for the privilege to continue being a cherished wife, mother, and fan!

The willingness of Kathi and her family to share their story has been an inspiration to us and we are honored to nominate Kathi for this once in a lifetime opportunity.]

Wow! What kind words. Although Mom was not given this once in a lifetime opportunity to meet the donor, she was still grateful for having been given a second chance at life. May 29, 2010 was extra special for me. The morning of my wedding, I counted my blessings. Not only was I about to marry the man of my dreams, but also my mother was going to be there by my side.

I knew it would be a long day for my mom, but that did not stop her. First thing in the morning, she was by my side at the salon getting her hair and makeup done. We found an amazing stylist David, who was with Mom each step of the way as she grew her hair back. He had seen Mom's baldhead, fixed up her wigs, and on that special day, had hair to work with. He worked wonders and styled her hair so that she looked like herself again. Mom looked beautiful. I was so happy to see her, her own hair and her own eyelashes done up. She stayed the entire time at the salon sitting next to me, while we sipped mimosas.

From the salon, we went back to the bridal suite to get dressed. We had found Mom a gorgeous mother of the bride dress that was so soft it felt like a nightgown. Mom looked perfect; she even wore a bit of a high heel, something she had not worn for years. I slipped into my gown with the help of my maid of honor and bridesmaids.

Only brides, who have had a parent fight and beat cancer would know how extra special this day was for me. I know traditionally, the father of the bride walks his daughter down the aisle. This was not the case for me. My dad understood when I asked him if he would mind if Mom joined us on that walk. May 29, 2010 at St. Frances DeSales Catholic Church, I took Mom on one arm and Dad on the other and "just the three of us" walked down the aisle to Brian. I could not have been any happier. Brian and I had a large wedding party consisting of our best friends. We had all seven of Aunt Barbara's little ones participate, two as my junior bridesmaids and the rest as the "communion crew." Angie and Julie passed out communion. It meant the world to me to have them all involved. The church was packed with friends and family. As I held Brian's hands getting ready to say our vows, I got extremely choked up and couldn't go on. I threw my right pointer finger up in the air and paused, asking for a timeout to get it together. Brian, held my hands, rubbed them, and helped me calm down. I was crying because I was overwhelmed by emotion. I was getting ready to marry the man of my dreams, my mom was finally healthy again, and at the same time, I was missing many loved ones who I wish could have been there. Right before I said my vows, I had a personal moment that until now, I had kept to myself. As I was trying to pull myself together, a beautiful white bird, possibly a dove, flew by the glass church window I was looking out. This bird gave me the strength to continue. Some may call me crazy, but I have always wondered, was it my Grandpa Hahn looking down at me, my Nanny, Aunt Barbara? So many loved ones who I knew were watching over me, proud, yet wishing they could be there. That moment gave me a sense of calmness from head to toe. I took a deep breath, looked Brian in the eyes and vowed to be his wife. With this, we exchanged rings, and the rest seems like it flew by, before we even knew it, Father Leon was pronouncing us man and wife, Mr. and Mrs. Brian Calvery!

Just the three of us!

The day was perfect. Then we were off to celebrate. The party began!!! From the church, we went to the reception where Mom did it! She danced at my wedding. I clearly remember the band playing my parents' song, Through the Years by Kenny Rogers. My mom and my dad went out and danced to it, bringing many tears of joy to everyone. I am not sure if there was a dry eye in the house. The nearly 200 guests had all eyes on my parents. I watched from the side, Brian had his arm wrapped around me, and just teared-up thinking of how far she had come, and how she had fought for our family. That moment was her triumphant finish line, a goal from day one. In addition to the unbelievable dance, my dad gave an amazing speech too, which not only expressed how happy and proud he was of me on my wedding day, but how the woman he married 35 years ago was by his side and healthy yet again! She met her goal and we knew from then on, nothing would stand in her way of getting back to being 100%!!!

CHAPTER 26: JUNE 2010- ROAD TO A NORMAL LIFE AGAIN

"Believe that life is worth living and your belief will help create the fact." – William James

June 2, 2010
Subject: Hahn Update- First Glimpse 6-2-10

An update from Mom...She wrote this I am just sending it out for her:

WE DID IT !!!!! I was able to dance at Ashley's wedding. That has been my goal through these last 2 difficult years. I owe a special thank you to all of you for the prayers, cards, good wishes and help. Whenever there was a moment of doubt or self pity one of you pulled me through. WE DID IT !!!!! Thank you all.

-Love, Kathi

A note from me:

So, for those of you who remember, Mom's goal going into all of this chaos two years ago was to dance at my wedding which she did this past Saturday!!! AND, she even did it with her own hair....no wig :)

Attached are only a few pictures from the day....I will post more once my photographer gets back to me.

Big Hugs!

Ash

For "normal people," recovering from an immediate family member's wedding may take a few days, clearing your system of all of the alcohol, resting up after long days leading up to the wedding and the feeling of being emotionally drained. For Mom, it took over a week! She was exhausted, but was still on cloud nine!

June 9, 2010
Subject: Hahn Update-June 9

Clear the roads! Mom got great news today from her eye doctor. He does not need to see her until September and the procedure he had done to her several months ago really looks like it is holding up and looks good. Again, he says she can see, but she still isn't quite up to speed with him. He thinks she is able to start to drive short distances, so we will be taking Mom to the parking lot to get her back behind the wheel...two years of being her chauffeur.....I can't wait!!! :) J/K mom!!! The doc said she could have another surgery to remove a cataract anytime she wanted hoping to improve her vision even more, but he also said no rush...she could do it tomorrow or she could do it in five years. She is not jumping to have it anytime soon.

Big hugs to all!
Ash

Talk about a role reversal at that time. Mom and Dad spent a long time teaching me how to drive at the age of 16. Then, at 60, Mom was going to have to relearn how to drive. If you happen to find yourself in a situation where you haven't driven yourself anywhere in a very long time, no need to worry! Mom said it was just like riding a bike. Once you get back on, you know just what to do. She did great on our first trip down to the big church parking lot by our house. I watched her like a hawk, making sure she used her turn signal, mirrors, etc. I was scared that she would have forgotten her basic driving skills as a result of her "chemo brain." Instead, she did just fine. Since she did so well in the large, vacant parking lot, I decided to let her take an outing onto the road. I had her drive us a block from the parking lot to the gas station.

That little trip made Mom feel so good again. She had some freedom back! She knew with a little more practice, and a boost of confidence, she could start to get out and about again without having to wait for a ride. She would no longer be a hostage in her own house!

CHAPTER 27: JULY AND AUGUST 2010- FIRST SUMMER POST-TRANSPLANT

Rapper, Eminem sings, "The truth is you don't know what is going to happen tomorrow. Life is a crazy ride, and nothing is guaranteed."

July 7, 2010
Subject: Hahn Update-July 7 doc visit and donor letter

Good news from the Hahns :)

Mom saw Dr. Craig today and he gave her another 2 months off! Her numbers looked good and he decided to keep her on all of the same meds. He was pleased with how she looked and the only bit of bad news he gave her was that her next apt, Sept 1, she will be getting her first round of baby shots :(She will need 5 in her visit....she needs to be re-vaccinated since we don't know what her lady had and Mom's whole immune system was wiped out pre-transplant. Crazy huh?!? Also, Dr. C has given Mom permission to sit out in the sun a little bit at a time if she wears sunscreen.

More good news...Mom and I picked up her prescription glasses today. I keep calling her sunglasses, the ones she is supposed to use to help her see when driving, her "miracle glasses." They are unreal. She put them on and was reading signs before I could even begin to make out what they said. I told her that they made for good news and bad. Good, that we can get her back on the road and behind the wheel b/c now she can finally see, and bad, because I didn't know how blind she was when she was driving...uh oh!!! We plan on practicing a little tomorrow in a parking lot and again next week when I am home.

Lastly, we will not know more about Mom's second nomination to meet her donor for a little while. The deadline to submit the entry was July and the actual convention is in November. They are worried Mom's donor came from a 2 yr registry which would mean we need to wait until February before they can meet in person...we will wait and see, fingers crossed though that they choose Mom's story. In the meanwhile, Mom got another letter from the donor.....I will type it verbatim below.

Love to all,
Ash

Donor Letter:

Hallo,

Thank you very for the wonderful card. I was very happy about it. I am very sorry that I am answering so late but since December I have been working on my new job, I work 40 hours every week and the three children, the housework, but my husband tries to help me everywhere he can do. On April 11th my son had his kindergarten communion and we celebrated it with 30 persons, it was very nice, also exhausting.

So now the important part. How are you? I think very much about you and your family. When you achieve this card then the marriage ceremony will be probably over. We wish you all the best and happiness....I am looking forward to hearing from you. I think and pray for you!

In love.....

What a treat it was to walk into the doctor's office and receive a good report. Not only did we receive great news from the doctor, we were also met by the transplant coordinator who gave us a card from the donor. These letters were always very special for Mom as well as our family. Since Mom's reports from Dr. Craig were getting better and better, less and less emails were going out to friends and family. That was a good thing!

August 30, 2010
Subject: Hahn Update August 30

Hey all! I am sure you have missed me :)

Mom went to see her main doc, Dr. Craig today. Even though she got 5 shots (her first round of baby immunizations that she had to get), he gave her great news again!!! WOOHOO!!!! :)

Her counts all looked good and he took away a few more pills. The best news though was that he gave her 2 full months off. She was ecstatic :)

Other updates...her eyes remain the same, but she can see well with the special prescription sunglasses/everyday glasses she ordered. She is driving again and loves the freedom to just go to the grocery store on her own. She is even guilty of driving herself for a mani/pedi :)

I am sooo proud of her. She pushes herself to do a little more and more everyday, often taking two walks in the neighborhood, running her own errands again, and back doing all of the laundry/ironing and cooking!!!

Thanks again for all of your prayers and support!

Love to all!
Ash

CHAPTER 28: FALL AFTER TRANSPLANT

"After climbing a great hill, one only finds that there are many more hills to climb." –Nelson Mandela

Good news from Dr. Craig did not always mean good news all around. In September, Mom had a not so fun visit with Dr. Jabbour, her eye specialist.

September 12, 2010
Subject: Hahn Update-Sept 12

Unfortunately, last Wednesday Mom went to the eye specialist and on her "good eye," right then and there he performed a laser procedure. He told her the retina was thinning and that it was best to nail it down now before it tears. Dr. Jabbour did this right on the spot and Mom went home, blind in both eyes. The good news is within hours her sight came back in that eye and she went in Friday for a check up and all looked good. He said he would see her in three weeks. Just a little bump in the road, but she is all right. Brian and I will be making our way to WV Saturday for the MD vs. WV football game....who to cheer for.....the terps or the eers?!? Mom is excited...she has been getting to the games and has even been able to walk up to the parking lot, which is up a steep hill and has to climb a million stairs to get there. Dad told me last game she got half way and said, "am I getting close?" He just kept telling her...don't look up, just keep walking!!! She's a trooper!!!

Love to all
Ash

Another punch, but it didn't knock my mom down. Mom had the procedure and moved on. We were able to go to the football game and she was able to see well enough to cheer on the Mountaineers. We got to witness Mom on the steps up the big hill. She did great! I was the one asking if we could take a breather on each landing. Boy, had I gotten out of shape the last couple of years.

October 27, 2010
Subject: Hahn Update-October 27th

Mom got good news this week so I thought I would share!!! :)

She saw the eye specialist who told her things looked good (one eye is almost perfect, the other she still can't see a thing) but somehow things look good. He was pleased with her eyes and gave her 2 months off...yippee!!!

Then today, she saw Dr. Craig who told her that all of her numbers looked great and he had nothing to say to her, which is awesome! She does not need to go back until January!

This is awesome news. She continues to drive herself around, run errands, takes daily walks, goes to football games and is anxiously awaiting the bball season which will be here before we know it!

This Halloween marks 3 years since ovarian cancer and February 6th marks 2 years post transplant!!! Sooooo proud of you Mom!!!!!

Love to all
Ash

It was amazing that because of the leukemia and bone marrow transplant the time flew by since the ovarian diagnosis. We were grateful to be approaching the 3-year mark from the ovarian cancer and the 2-year transplant   birthday.

CHAPTER 29: WINTER

Jon Bon Jovi said, "Believe in love. Believe in magic. Hell, believe in Santa Clause. Believe in others. Believe in yourself. Believe in your dreams. If you don't, who will?"

December 21, 2010
Subject: Hahn Update Dec. 21st

Hey everyone!

Just a brief update. Mom went to the eye specialist the other day and he thought things looked good. She was given 3 months off from seeing him. This is great news! Eventually, he still wants to do the cataract surgery but is in no rush. She still says she is blind though :(

Mom continues to drive herself around, run errands, and hasn't missed one of Dad's games yet. She even made the trip to Puerto Rico for the November basketball tournament without her nurse (me!)....I was proud but very jealous.

We hope you have a very Merry Christmas and a Happy New Year! This is the first year in a long time our whole family will be together on Christmas day. It is so nice to have Matt in the Pittsburgh area close to home :)

Love to all
Ash

Yes, you read that update correctly. I did not go to Puerto Rico with Mom and the team. It was a very hard trip for me because we were roaming on our cell phone coverage, so we could only check in every few days. Remember, I talk to my mom and dad every day about ten times a day and for her to be that far away, I was worried. She did great though and had an amazing time.

December 28, 2010
Subject: Hahn Update Dec. 28-good and bad

Some good news and bad news. Since I got home for the holidays I decided to play nurse Hahn and check up on Mom. Dad told me to take a peek at her legs b/c he noticed that she developed a little rash. Well....after looking, I didn't like what I saw...not one bit. I got right on the phone and set up an appointment with Dr. Craig (Mom was scheduled to see him Monday but I wanted to be here for it). His office called us this morning and told us to be there by 2.

Bad news: Mom officially has Graft Versus Host Disease of the skin (this is the dreaded GVHD we did NOT want her to get).

Good news: Dr. Craig said this was to be expected. He did not seem very concerned and said it was mild. He gave us two options...one would be to just wait and see what happens and the other was to apply a topical steroid to the area for 3-4 weeks. We decided we have attacked everything before and we would again, so we went with the steroid cream. I asked Dr. Craig if it was something to worry about and he said, "no." He wants to see what the cream does the next several weeks and will see Mom again at the end of January. At that time, if it seems worse, then he will switch her over to an oral steroid....BUT.....he thinks this first option may work. Prayers needed again.

Other than this, Mom is doing wonderful! We have been running like crazy, shopping, eating out and having a great few days together. Tomorrow opens the Big East season for Dad...we will be at the game cheering him on! Go Eers!!!

Hope you don't hear from me until the end of January and hope it is great news then. Have a Healthy, Happy New Year!!!!
Love to all,
Ashley

We had another Christmas with a lot to celebrate. It was wonderful having all of us together even if it was a short period of time. We were lucky to have Mom back. We laughed again as we opened presents because everyone knew what they were getting. I was Santa again that year and did the shopping for Mom on her credit card. I asked everyone what he or she wanted and needed and that is exactly what he or she got. Although no surprises, it was a very special Christmas.

February 2, 2011
Subject: Hahn Update Feb 2nd

Mom's 2nd birthday is just around the corner!!! This Sunday, February 6th marks her two-year anniversary post-transplant. To make the celebration even brighter, she saw Dr. Craig today and got a great report! All of her lab work came back with good numbers and her GVHD (skin rash) looked better. He told her she could continue to treat it with the lotion as needed. He seemed happy she was doing so well and they had more time socializing than talking about her health :)
When she was at the office today they even asked her to speak at a conference sometime soon at the Greenbrier Hotel/Casino...she jumped all over it :)
Things are going well. Thanks again for your ongoing support.

Big hugs to all!
Ash

Little did Mom know that behind her back I was throwing another little surprise gathering for her 2nd birthday. I invited a few close friends and all of our "neighbor ladies" who had been with us each step of the way. We had a great turnout and she was so surprised.
February 6th was extra special. Mom turned 2! Mom was glowing on that day. She was extra-smiley and had a unique bounce in her step. I look forward to celebrating many more birthdays with Mom and someday meeting the woman who saved her life. The last checkup with Dr. Craig that I want to mention was on February 8, 2011, when Mom was given extraordinary news. Her numbers looked great and she was officially still 100% donor. A huge success!

A picture from Mom's second birthday.

CHAPTER 30: A NEW BEGINNING

Semisonic made a song with the lyrics, "Every new beginning comes from some other beginning's end."

This was a true story about my mom the miracle: one woman, two cancers, and three years of her life, who is forever grateful to a total stranger! It's hard to believe that as I finish writing this book my mom is 2 ½ years post-transplant. She is amazing! From worrying about losing my mom to cancer, to picking her up at the Fort Lauderdale International Airport in Florida, I couldn't be any prouder. There really is such a thing as a happy ending! I love you, Mom!

One last reminder to those going through this "hell," keep on fighting and don't ever lose faith. You too, could be writing a book one day about the ruthless journey you had that made you appreciate everyday a little more. Go get 'em and keep your head held high! Big hugs! –Ash

The End, or should I say, "Just the Beginning of a New Chapter."

2009-Group picture from the outpatient center

2010- Wedding Photo

2011-Mom's first trip to Florida!

Made in the USA
Charleston, SC
26 March 2014